Istanbul - 2013

© Erkam Publications 2013 / 1434 H

Erkam Publications
İkitelli Organize Sanayi Bölgesi Mahallesi Atatürk Bulvarı
Haseyad 1.Kısım No: 60 / 3-C Başakşehir / İSTANBUL
Tel: (90-212) 671-0700 pbx
Fax: (90-212) 671-0717
E-mail: info@islamicpublishing.net
Web site: http://www.islamicpublishing.net

All rights reserved. No part of this publication may be reproduced, stored in a retrieval system, or transmitted in any from or by any means, electronic, mechanical, photocopying, recording or otherwise, without the prior permisson of the copyright owner.

ISBN: 978-9944-83-370-7

The author	: Osman Nûri Topbaş
Translator	: İsmail Eriş
Copy Editor	: Süleyman Derin
Graphics	: Rasim Şakiroğlu (Worldgraphics)
Printed by	: Erkam Printhouse

A PEACEFUL HOME

Paradise on Earth

Osman Nûri TOPBAŞ

ERKAM
PUBLICATIONS

FOREWORD

All praise is due to Allah, who created humanity from a male and a female and opened our hearts to the love of divine majesty.

And peace and blessings be upon our eminent guide Muhammad Mustafa, who prepared our hearts for the love of Allah the Almighty and lived the most perfect and ideal example of family life.

Certainly there is love in the creation of all beings.

Before the creation of the worlds, Allah the Almighty was *"a hidden treasure."* He *"loved to be known,"* and so created all existence. Divine love is therefore the essence of all love and Allah the Almighty has bestowed all other types of love as preparatory and elevating steps toward divine love. He created the love and affection between man and woman as the most valuable means to reach the apex of His love. And He made the family, which is established by a marriage contract in His name, as the most meaningful and blessed place of manifestation for human love and affection.

Family, in this respect, is an indispensible means for reaching at the love of Allah as well as a divine dispensation for the continuance of the generations. The family environment both addresses our physical needs and serves as an essential ground for our spiritual development. For this reason the religious thinkers of Islam have always regarded marriage as essential and have highly encouraged it. Since celibacy is against the nature of most human beings, if there is no obstacle, humans should not avoid the married state. Marriage is an important custom of the Prophet.

Because starting a family has such great importance, it should be undertaken with forethought. There are many significant and delicate matters that need to be taken into consideration if we hope to obtain the desired results and turn our family environment into a peaceful paradise.

What should be done in order to start a family that can act as a step toward divine love? What principles should we follow in order to turn our homes into gardens of peace and tranquility? How might we live so that our family's life journey ends in eternal union? How might we obtain a happiness that will continue beyond this world, into the life to come?

In the world we live in, the answers to these vital questions are not common knowledge. Fortunately, the religious thinkers of Islam have given the situation much thought. Our tradition has elaborately

Foreword

regulated methods, principles, guidelines and measures, all of which can help us to realize the most desired objects of family life. It has also pointed out the grave and unfortunate results if these guidelines are not followed.

To help us toward ideal success in the cultivation of a peaceful family, Allah the Almighty has given us the best and most perfect example, the Sultan of Souls, Muhammad Mustafa (peace and blessings be upon him). Our Prophet, who had not even the smallest negativity in his life, lived these principles at the highest level in his own family. For this reason we would do well to study his life, which is full of honorable and exceptional beauties and take it as our model in the establishment of a good family. If we neglect this inspiration, our society may well fall into crisis for lack of warm, peaceful and blessed homes.

We observe that many young couples in our society, who are unsuccessful in starting a properly balanced family, end up with unhappy divorce, thus darkening not just their own but also their children's world. Worse, many heedless people now stay away from marriage altogether and find themselves torn apart by the vortex of sin.

We hope that the booklet before you may prove a beneficial ointment for the wounds of our society. It contains a collection of interviews originally published in *Şebnem* magazine, but there have been some additions and expansions made.

In this work you will find basic Islamic principles and information for establishing a peaceful home. It explains the required guidelines and measures for setting up a family and gives related examples, particularly emphasizing examples from the life our Master (peace and blessings be upon him) and from the lives of other respected Muslim figures. We have our readers' clear understanding and better comprehension always in mind.

We ask and pray that Allah the Almighty may make this modest work beneficial both for couples who have already established a home and for those who are planning to start one.

May Our Lord help us to establish and maintain strong families in this contemporary age in which families are torn apart, in which immorality and hate have spread like a disease! May our home be a paradise of peace and tranquility! And may the last gate of this paradise open upon the eternal Paradise where union with the beauty of Allah the Almighty manifests!

Amin!

Marriage and Family in Islam

Marriage is the path of the prophets, the custom of the Messenger of Allah (peace and blessings be upon him), the wellspring of new generations, the honor of man and woman, the castle of chastity and the privilege of human beings over the rest of creation.

Q - We might begin by asking: Do people have to live socially and start families at all? Can't they just as well live alone?

Being alone is only truly appropriate for Allah the Almighty. The Creator has reserved oneness for Himself alone, while He has created all of existence in pairs. Thus all creatures are in need of each other and at the same time, since they are created, they have intrinsic deficiency and weakness in their nature. *Ma siwa Allah,* "the other-than-Allah" — all beings except Allah the Almighty — are continuously in need of both each other and Allah the Almighty.

Out of all creation, human beings need each other the most. People have so many needs and requests, compared to other beings! Because people always want to live in material and spiritual comfort, their needs constantly increase and never come to an end. Problems, privation, pains, sufferings and disasters all present us with difficulties. In times of trouble, we look for a soul to take shelter with and a hand to hold.

Thus the descendant of Adam is indicated in Arabic by the word *insan*, which is derived from the word *uns* or *unsiyya*, meaning intimacy. Even philology demonstrates our need to be close to our fellows! This need is our first quality and humans are distinguished by this quality.

The clearest manifestation of intimacy is the togetherness that joins a man and a woman. This matter is necessary, even obligatory, for the continuance of human generations.

The necessity of togetherness manifests itself in living beings through the existence of males and females and in inanimate beings though the existence of positive and negative poles. This situation is stated in the Qur'an in many verses:

"And of everything We have created pairs: that ye may receive instruction." (51: 49)

"Glory to Allah, Who created in pairs all things that the earth produces, as well as their own (human) kind and (other) things of which they have no knowledge." (36:36)

"And (have We not) created you in pairs?" (78: 8)

To possess the nature of being created in pairs means to be created as man and woman, complementary, not in twos of the same kind. In such a case, the creation of one of the two would be redundant and redundancy cannot be attributed to Allah the Almighty. Therefore Allah created the creation in gendered couples. Yet each individual created is unique in itself. Allah does not create duplicate beings, exactly the same. Even identical twins have many physical and spiritual differences.

So Allah the Almighty created all beings in complementary pairs and simultaneously placed His divine law of attraction between them in order to make them come closer to each other. For He has assigned the spiritual and material development of all these pairs to the unification possible between them.

Although the need and attraction a man feels toward a woman and a woman toward a man essentially serve the continuance of progeny, this is not their only purpose. One of their most significant functions is to form the basis for stable families, which create an environment that allows individuals to achieve spiritual and social peace and balance. This goal can be achieved only through *mahabbat Allah,* the inclination of the heart to Allah the Almighty with love.

At times the love for God can be attained through earthly love: the lover ascends from Laila (the archetypal human beloved) to Mawla (the Lord – the divine beloved). But for this journey to be possible, there has to be a Leila in the first place! Then love between a man and a woman may constitute the first step in coming closer to Allah. Even if attraction begins with the arousal of selfish desires, it cannot turn into true human love until it is freed from the selfishness of those desires. When the mutual beholding of divine attributes is manifested in the lovers, only then do we call attraction, love.

The heart, which is the subtle center of attraction, is exercised and strengthened through couples' affection for each other and thus gains capacity for the love of Allah. The ability to sustain Divine love is further developed through love for one's children, the natural fruit of a family.

In order to be encompassed by love for Allah, a marriage must be founded upon divine principles. A marriage undertaken purely for the sake of carnal desires and inclinations usually does not create love. The spiritual development and training of the heart through love that may be expected from an Islamic marriage cannot be realized in families established on lust alone, because in such marriages couples become slaves. Forget spiritual progress: such couples may even lose the spiritual levels they had enjoyed while single.

A desirable marriage is one which matures us and helps us to spiritually improve. A marital relationship that functions in such a way manifests an ideal perfection. It is this kind of marriage that is called, in the traditions of the Prophet (peace and blessings be upon him), "half of religion." Attaining half of something does not mean we give up seeking the other half. We should do everything we can to realize the ideal attributes of a marriage. Only then can we achieve the maturity, peace and tranquility we aim for.

Marriage and Family in Islam

Although intimate relationship between a man and a woman is one way to achieve the capacity for Divine love, it is not the only way. Single people can and do make spiritual progress. There are many pious single people mentioned in the Qur'an, starting with Mary[1] and Jesus (may Allah be pleased with them). This fact confirms that not everybody is created with the same natural abilities. Environment, too, has differing effects on people. In some people's destiny the paths to marriage are closed; obstacles preventing marriage may constitute a divine test for them. For others, marriage can be a source of suffering and disappointment. Allah the Almighty bestows certain special capabilities upon those servants who endure such tests and through these capabilities they can ob-

---

1. The name of Mary is mentioned in the Qur'an 34 times and also 23 times as part of the phrase "Jesus son of Mary." In addition, the nineteenth chapter of the Qur'an is named after her. She is the only woman who is mentioned in the Qur'an by her personal name. Some of the wise intentions behind this special treatment, as divined by Qur'anic exegetes, include:
   1. The previously debased image of women was exalted through our mother Mary.
   2. Her being continually mentioned as the mother of one of the greatest prophets shows the value given to motherhood in Islam.
   3. The emphasis on the chastity of our mother Mary shows the importance of protecting the chastity of women; protecting chastity is obligatory in Islam.
   4. Distinctive feminine virtues are highlighted through Mary's personality. Though her we learn that qualities such as chastity, dignity, patience, submission, resistance and courage, are characteristics elevating the station of women before Allah the Almighty.

tain the spiritual benefits to be expected from a normal marriage. Some single servants of Allah made great spiritual progress through their mercy and compassion to animals and plants. Others ascended the steps of spirituality by bearing with the tests of their marriages. The Companions of the Bench, who comprised Companions of the Prophet who were too poor to get married, reached the peaks of spirituality through knowledge and learning. It should not be forgotten, however, that these are exceptional and special cases. The general rule is that human beings should get married and start a happy family.

It is a fact that a heart without love and affection is like an unplanted field, left idle for a long time. The relationship between man and woman will cultivate this land. Of course, to be successful, such a relationship cannot be based on selfish desires. Success can be achieved only by getting rid of selfish motives. As we have said, an intimate natural relationship must turn its direction to divine love, because only when the connection between man and woman attains this divine quality do souls ascend in the love for Allah. To have children in this state constitutes the second level in reaching the love for Allah. Next comes love for relatives, friends, teachers and others. So the heart matures, step by step drawing closer to its highest goal, divine love. After becoming one with divine love, a servant joins the friends of Allah the Almighty. This is the purpose of the creation of humanity.

In short, our need for family and for togetherness between man and woman is a reality embedded in our natures by our Creator in order to realize a lofty goal. The more we realize this goal, the more the tree of family branches out, bearing sweet fruits of social peace, tranquility and balance.

Therefore the establishment of a peaceful family environment comes at the head of the list of the most important endeavors for raising society to a civilized level. Man and woman make their pledges to each other in the name of Allah the Almighty because that promise marks their intention to make love a reality in accordance with of the purpose of their creation. Of course mutual respect, trust and sincerity must nurture their efforts!

Q - What do the traditions of Islam say about family?

Because of the aforementioned reasons, the thinkers of Islam have attributed great significance to family. Families are like the seeds of a society. As a matter of historical fact, families built on strong bases protect and embellish the structure of their society, while families established by spiritually unequal partners, destroy it.

The principles and measures of Islam work to establish a happy and balanced family. One might say that Islam aims at peace and tranquility through family. That is why it is said that "home is the Paradise of the living." As a matter of fact, a home set up according to divine rules is like Paradise on earth.

Because such a noble ideal and institution can only be achieved through exalted measures and lawful foundations based on love, Islam begins this spiritual journey with mutual vows. Islamic law requires both parties to give certain promises to each other in the name of Allah the Almighty.

The old saying "marriage works miracles" points out the significance and benefits of the marriage agreement in establishing a peaceful family. The value of our acts depends on our intentions. The outcome of living as partners without being married, without an explicit exchange of vows expressing our intentions, is disappointment and collapse not only on the personal level but also at the level of society as a whole. That is why cohabitation without a marriage agreement is prohibited by Islam and accepted as one of the grave sins. There will be harsh divine punishment for such practices in the Hereafter.

Q – Since marriage is so significant, could you please elaborate the issue a little more?

Marriage is the way of the prophets, the custom of the Messenger of Allah (peace be upon them), the dignity of man and woman and the privilege of human beings over other creatures.

It is necessary to have two male witnesses to a marriage agreement in order to announce it to society. The togetherness of man and woman is the basic element of socialization and so the onset of this togetherness should be made known to the public. Demonstrating our intentions does not always require having witnesses; however, witnesses are required for a marriage agreement in order to make the union an accepted fact throughout the community. A single man or woman may always receive proposals. But when a couple announces their marriage, proposals stop and the spouses commence to belong to each other. This is the foundation of a healthy family and a healthy society. That is why there is a usually a wedding feast: it makes the whole community witness to the marriage, even though two formal witnesses are sufficient for the contract to be valid. Marriage ceremonies are celebrated not just to share the joy of the marrying couple, but also to declare their status to the community. So we see that the marriage agreement, with all its features, is a divine command intended to protect human dignity.

According to Islam, marriage is the indispensible foundation of a family. It furthers the raising of progeny, their formation and discipline, as well as the conservation of the values and dignity of humanity. Islam gives such great importance to this foundation that it refuses all miserable and contemptible relations attacking it. In this respect Islam prohibits adultery, which is the worst of all out-of-wedlock relations, because adultery is an attack on the refinement, beauty and legality of the marriage agreement, as well as being a cruel crime, which destroys progeny. There cannot be a more foolish and ignorant act than preferring the indecency of adultery over the peaceful and tranquil world of marriage. Hence, the streets of a country should not be polluted with scenes of immorality glorifying this disaster.

It should not be forgotten that the basis upon which a nation stands or falls is the strength of its moral and ethical structure. The marriage agreement is the most effective method of protecting this structure. For this reason, the Messenger of Allah (peace and blessings be upon him) warned Muslims not to make marriage difficult, saying: *"The best marriages are those which are most simple."* (Abu Dawud, *Nikah*, 32) Therefore all customary expenses which load an additional burden on a marriage agreement are completely null and void; they are the remnants of the age of ignorance before Islam.

Allah the Almighty wants His servants to live in chastity and tranquility. The most effective way to protect chastity is marriage. Those who have enough means to marry should marry and the Muslim community has the responsibility to help those who do not have the means to get married. This is stated in the following verse:

Marriage and Family in Islam

"And marry those among you who are single and those who are fit among your male slaves and your female slaves; if they are needy, Allah will make them free from want out of His grace; and Allah is Ample-giving, Knowing." (24:32)[2]

In the Ottoman Empire, special religious foundations were established for this purpose. Their founders were well aware that the morality and order of a society depend on chaste and peaceful individuals.

Muhyiddin ibn 'Arabi (may Allah bless his soul) says about the merits of assisting people to get married: "The best continuous charity is to help people to get married; because for those who help, there will be a share in the rewards of the good deeds of the progeny of the couples they helped to get married."

The family life which began with Adam and Eve (peace and blessings be upon them) in Paradise has been transferred to the children of Adam through the divine laws of marriage and Islam has made this explicit. As a matter of fact Islam set some specific principles for family life and thus brought the peace of Paradise into its families. In order to attain such happiness, we should abide by the rules of Allah

---

2. For English translation of the verses, I have benefited from Shakir, M.H. (trans.), *The Qur'an [al-Qur'an al-ḥakim]*, Elmhurst, N.Y.: Tahrike Tarsile Qur'an, 1997 and Pickthall, M. W. (trans.), *The Meaning of the Glorious Koran: An Explanatory Translation*, New York, N.Y.: Dorset Press, 1988.

the Almighty and live our family life like Adam and Eve. We should embrace each other with love and be of one soul and one heart, as our father Adam and mother Eve were.

Though we often treat it lightly, there are deep wisdoms in the amazing union that takes place between two strangers through the act of marriage. Two young souls leave their parents' house and grow attached to each other with a love and affection set by Allah in their hearts. What a lofty divine manifestation it is, to see such an incredible closeness develop between two strangers! The mystery of it is indeed a sacred lesson, deserving of contemplation.

Allah the Almighty has made marriage a gate of blessings for the Muslim community and He makes each marriage established according to Qur'an and Sunna a paradise of happiness on earth.

Islam, which aims to create a dignified life for humanity, gives the highest importance to women and points out the possible problems if they are neglected. Women are like crystal chandeliers. When their marriage experience is full of blessings and light, they illuminate society. They protect the dignity and chastity of family. They stand like lighthouses against the whirlpools of sin. When things are otherwise, whole generations are lost. Losing generations breaks the bonds of interpersonal relations and the transmission of wisdom; the process ends in the destruction of a society. Mischief becomes common;

sensitive and humane feelings cease to exist. Troubles and scandals rise up. These are all signs of a community in collapse.

Women's happiness is made possible when marriage is gentle. When it is not, a woman sometimes looks elsewhere. If a woman directs herself away from her principal object, her unhappiness will destroy peaceful family life. A woman's participation in the employment world follows necessity; if she works, she needs to work at a job that suits her nature. The degree of necessity should be judged objectively, with the needs of the whole community taken into consideration. Employment must be within reasonable and lawful limits. Anything else is self-deception, which ends in disappointment and frustration. Many Muslim girls have been lost to the whirlpools of heedlessness. Many eyes, deceived by illusory worldviews, have been blinded to divine truth and destroyed their own possibilities for happiness.

The religious thinkers of Islam have tied women's moral and social identity and glory to their marital welfare. Woman enters into a whole new world through marriage. Maybe she begins to live with a complete stranger, maybe with his relatives. However, with the special blessing bestowed upon marriage by Allah, these two stranger souls become so attached to each other that they become the closest people in the world. In fact it is stated in the following verse that:

"And one of His signs is that He created mates for you from yourselves that you may find rest in them and He put between you love and compassion; most surely there are signs in this for a people who reflect." (30:21)

Therefore, the most important factor for happiness in a family is the love, sincerity and mercy that exist between husband and wife.

> *Q- It is not always possible to attain such happiness in all families. It is a sign of great blessing to reach this happiness and tranquility. Yet if we hope to reach this level of happiness, what should we be careful about?*

The first condition is to follow Islamic guidelines for selecting a suitable spouse. The essence of these guidelines is that believers should not select their spouses based on the temporary beauties of this world, like physical appearance and wealth. Instead, their selection must be based on spiritual qualities such as faith and morality. In this respect, the Prophet (peace and blessings be upon him) says:

"A woman is married for four things: her wealth, her family status, her beauty and her religion. Try to marry the one who is religious; may your hand be scented with goodness!" (Bukhari, *Nikah*, VI, 123; Muslim, *Rada*, 53)

Even though this tradition is about the qualities of an ideal wife, it is also applicable for choosing an ideal husband, because to have a righteous spouse is the second most valuable thing for every Muslim to have, after piety. A righteous husband is the unshakable pillar of the family palace and a righteous wife is the most valuable adornment of that palace. This is expressed in the following saying of the Prophet (peace and blessings be upon him):

"People's rank is hidden in their religion; their dignity is hidden in their reason; and the beauty of their progeny is hidden in the goodness of their morality [protected by marriage]."

The second important thing is to be careful about is equivalence between the spouses. Equality must be assessed according to qualities such as wealth, manners and cultural levels. The steps after these two depend on maturity and willpower. Maturity develops through seeking perfection in faith and practice; willpower can be achieved through embracing the Divine Law's orders and prohibitions.

A peaceful family, in which the commands and prohibitions of Allah are observed, is the foundation of felicity in this world and one of the greatest blessings of our Lord. Continuation of this felicity and blessing is contingent upon togetherness of the spouses in a spiritual atmosphere, which relies on mutual understanding and willing sacrifices.

A Peaceful Home

In the present day, the most significant source of erosion of the traditional family is women who try to resemble men and men who try to resemble women. Allah the Almighty has bestowed different qualities upon men and women. These qualities are shaped in order to give all the ability to do their best in society. The natural qualities of the sexes, from their physical appearances to their spiritual features, are formed according to the responsibilities assigned to them by Allah the Almighty.

Men require spiritual and physical strength in order to provide for the family and to lead it. Women are not held responsible for the provision of livelihood. If they are forced to provide, it is oppression and hardship, because women are not created to earn a family's sustenance, but rather to raise and protect its children. However if the environment and conditions are suitable, then women can work in positions that are favorable to their natures, such as being a teacher at Qur'anic schools for girls, or a gynecologist.

It is their natural abilities that make men and women different but complementary to each other. When spouses transgress the limits of these characteristics, the family's felicity suffers.

We should also mention that male authority in the family does not give any man the right to use brute force and that female obedience should not be tantamount to slavery. If both man and woman pursue their traditional roles in accordance with the principles of Islam, there will be neither an oppressor nor an oppressed in the family.

A woman's defiance of her husband by violating the principles of chastity and obedience and a man's abuse of his authority for his selfish desires, can each destroy a family. A man may sometimes experience stressful circumstances during the day at work. When he does, it is not just his need but also his right to find an understanding and consoling wife at home. On the other hand, it is both the need and the right of a wife who waits for her husband at home all day long to find sympathy and warmth in him when he arrives. Each person in a family must know his or her rights and responsibilities in the presence of Allah the Almighty. The only principle that can maintain felicity and joy in a family is mutual love and respect.

We should not forget the saying of our ancestors, "The female bird builds the nest." Women do have a more effective role in protecting a family. That is why women's intuition, understanding and efforts in this regard carry more significance than men's. Allah has bestowed greater emotional wisdom and capability upon mothers than upon fathers.

İsmail Hakkı Bursevî says about the interpretation of the term "*al-tara'ib*" from Sura 86 of the Quran, "When a child falls into a stream, its mother jumps into the stream, no matter how dangerous it is and does everything she can to save her baby. The child's father, on the other hand, does not act like this. If there is no hope from the baby, its father just sits on the shore and weeps."

Of course, such heroism shows itself in mothers who have not lost their spiritual qualities. It is not seen in those heartless women who abandon their children in front of mosques or at the edges of cemeteries. They are like ruined souls who have destroyed all the good qualities of their creation.

The compassion of motherhood is visible even in the animal kingdom, sometimes remarkably so. It was recorded that a mother lion and a baby deer grew amazingly close to each other in Kenya's Samburu National Park between December 21, 2001 and January 2, 2002. Their relation was like that of a mother and child. The fawn's umbilical cord was still attached to it when its existence was first captured by cameras. Did the mother lion feel sorry for the lost baby deer? In any case, she adopted it. The fawn, too, behaved as if the lioness were its real mother. Because the fawn could not nurse on lion's milk, the mother lion was feeding it with green leaves, not meat – as if she recognized that it was not a lion cub.

Then the mother deer appeared, looking for her baby. When she saw her baby with a lion, she became confused, but she did not run. She started to make noises as if she were communicating with her baby. The baby deer came to her real mother and they grazed together. However, the mother lion did not allow them to go far away. If the deer started to move away, the lioness would intervene. Did the mother lion love the baby deer so much that she could not let it go with its real mother? She licked the fawn and played with it as if it were her own offspring. However after awhile, for some reason – maybe because she recognized that the baby deer needed its real mother – she let it go with the mother deer. Unfortunately it didn't take long for a male lion to notice the weak and unprotected fawn and kill it. The mother lion appeared to mourn by the place that the fawn was killed.

What an amazing scene this was! It was a great manifestation of the divine gift of motherhood overcoming even the natural enmity between predator and prey. This is one of the signs of Allah the Almighty, for motherhood is the manifestation of a divine miracle.

There are many lessons for us in this incident. A mother is a truly a mother not because of her physical qualities, but because of her spiritual qualities. If a woman gives up these spiritual qualities, then she is no longer a mother and a monument of mercy. Instead she becomes a hunter – and she destroys many young souls. Therefore women should value and protect the blessing of motherhood as more than simple animal reproduction. For other creatures there will be no questioning about their offspring in the Hereafter. But for humans, there will be.

Our children will count either for us or against us in the on the Day of Reckoning. They should be raised carefully, for they are means of entering Paradise. A good religious education, good manners, morality and consciousness of divine service come at the head of the things which should be taught to children.

> *Q - In our society, young people who plan to get married first spend time being engaged.. They face several problems during this period. What do the parties need to be careful about during their engagement?*

The central issue, as we have been trying to explain, is the necessity of building a family upon a strong and healthy foundation. This principle must be kept in mind not just during the engagement period, but in every phase of the establishment of the family. Divine rules and measure must be observed at every stage. Unfortunately, in our time some couples see the engagement as permission to act as if they were already married. This leads to a number of irreparable mistakes and to broken hearts.

We do need to remember that the engagement stage is just the period of agreement to marriage. It is not marriage itself and during the engagement period parties are still unlawful to each other. Therefore they must be careful about the divine limits. In short, engaged couples should not meet privately in secluded places and talk more than they are supposed to before the marriage! Today we witness the devastation caused by this type of carrying on.

In this regard I would like to remind you of the following narration of Ibn `Abbas:

Allah the Almighty created Eve from a rib from the left side of Adam. During her creation Adam (peace and blessings be upon him) was asleep. When he woke up and saw Eve next to him, he fell in love with her and wanted to hold her. Angels said, "O Adam! Do not touch her. You have not been married yet." Then they got married and for her marriage portion they agreed upon uttering three praises for the Prophet Muhammad (peace and blessings be upon him).

This was the beginning of the marriage agreement before Allah. Thus with the praise of the Prophet Muhammad (peace and blessings be upon him), the marriage agreement gains a sublime meaning and teems with blessings and manifestations of mercy.

> *Q – Would you share your observations about the marriage ceremony?*

The marriage ceremony is a means to share the happiness of a marriage with friends and relatives. It also serves as a way to carry out the requirement of publicizing a marriage. In addition, it is also a fine thing to turn such an important institution into an opportunity for joy and entertainment, which are part of our nature.

However, we should remember that ceremonies that are too extravagant, which reach the point of financially devastating the families involved, are never approved by Islam. Islam is a religion that urges moderation even in taking water from a river when performing ablution. It encourages its followers to be frugal. Therefore even if the parties are rich, they should act in consideration of the poor and needy of their community. Turning marriage ceremonies into theatres of ostentation, like many of today's rich families do, is a manifestation of madness and a proof that Islam is not properly internalized.

Marriage ceremonies should properly be performed with Islamic grace and refinement. They should stay away from every kind of lavishness. People should have modest ceremonies appropriate to their financial situations. But using the event as an opportunity to show off one's financial status contradicts the object and the spirit of a marriage ceremony.

In particular, to launch such a blessed institution with unlawful acts and customs, such as drinking alcohol, leads people to error and ignorance. Only those marriage gatherings which observe the laws of Allah and His Messenger are blessed places where prayers are accepted. Some types of entertainment are harmless, so long as the men and the women are not mixed. Women can entertain each other and men can do the same among themselves without committing any forbidden act.

Another significant issue is the importance of inviting poor, needy and homeless people to the *walima*, the marriage feast. This is expressed in the following hadith:

"The worst food is that of a wedding banquet to which only the rich are invited while the poor are not invited. And he who refuses an invitation (to a banquet) disobeys Allah and His Apostle." (Bukhari, *Nikah*, 72; Muslim, *Nikah*, 107. See also Ibn Maja, *Nikah*, 25)

It should be remembered that the Muslim community receives divine assistance because of the prayers of the weak. Therefore destitute and needy people particularly need to be invited to the *walima*. On one occasion Moses (peace and blessings be upon him) prayed to Allah the Almighty and asked, "Dear Lord! Where should I look for You?"

Allah the Almighty responded, "Look for Me by the broken hearts." (Abu Nu`aym, *Hilya*, II, 364)

The prayers of those who are destitute and have broken hearts are acceptable in the presence of Allah. This is why all Muslims should take care to merit their prayers, especially during those times when we begin an important undertaking like marriage.

Neither should we neglect to ask for the supporting prayers of the devout.

> Q - To what issues should young Muslim men and women pay particular attention in order to safeguard the soundness of their family?

We should know that a society rises on the shoulders of its male members, but that its female members also produce its ascension. Without the help of men and women alike, no development or ascent can be achieved. A man who is unhappy at home cannot be successful at work. Consequently we can say that a nation develops through the maturity and experience of its women. The opposite of this is also correct: a nation loses its power and value through the degradation of its female members. History teems with examples. That is why every community needs healthy families.

Although human beings are created with the most perfect of natures, the manifestation of our perfection in a developed personality can be achieved only in a healthy family environment. The family is the primary place where the human personality is educated. Only with a proper education can souls reach lofty spiritual states and stations. We can take lessons from the lives of the prophets and from the lives of the saints.

Marriage and Family in Islam

Felicity and joy in a family depend on mutual respect and understanding between the parties and on the observation of each other's rights. It is also very important to comprehend the meaning of the verse *ittaqu Allah* – "be mindful of Allah!"[3] – if happiness in the family is to be achieved.

Our world can become a paradise if the rights of women are observed; and it can also turn into a hell as a result of the violation of their rights. The Prophet (peace and blessings be upon him) expressed the significance of women's rights in his farewell sermon:

"O People, it is true that you have certain rights with regard to your women, but they also have rights over you. Remember that you have taken them as your wives only under Allah's trust and with His permission. If they abide by your right then to them belongs the right to be fed and clothed in kindness. Do treat your women well and be kind to them, for they are your partners and committed helpers. And it is your right that they do not make friends with anyone of whom you do not approve, as well as never to be unchaste."
(Bukhari, Mukhtasar, X, 398)

Preventing women from raising righteous generations by forcing them into unsuitable occupations is a great mistake. Happiness in a family can be achieved only by employing and protecting both men's and women's abilities in the occupations that best fulfill their natures.

---

3. Qur'an 2: 194

A Peaceful Home

Islam affirms the importance of marriages undertaken for the sake of lofty ideals. Marriage has two dimensions, worldly and spiritual. We must be serious and careful in order to make our families functional in both dimensions. It is all too easy for marriage to become one-dimensional. Unfortunately, this kind of marriage often ends up in an unhappy divorce, or continues as a chain of agony until the end of life. Naturally these are not the results we desire when getting married!

Divorce is depicted in one of the sayings of the Prophet as an incident which shakes Allah's throne:

"Marry and do not divorce, for verily divorce causes the throne of Allah to shake..." (`Ali al-Muttaqi, IX, 1161/27874)

For a man to divorce a woman merely for his own convenience and pleasure is oppression and great sin, which is certainly prohibited in Islam. It is violating another servant's right, which will lead to eternal disappointment and destruction.

Divorce often follows from arbitrarily and carelessly performed marriages and it has countless pitiful results. The worst and the severest of these results befall the children. Children who see no warmth in their families and are exposed to frequent abuses from their parents, who are supposed to be their role models, live at the mercy of the streets. Sometimes they run away from their homes and start living in the streets; they shortly fall into the web of alcohol, narcotics, prostitution and crime. This prepares the ground for social destruction.

Of course, there are times when divorce is the only reasonable option. Catholic marriages can never be annulled and must be continued no matter how miserable the parties are. Islamic marriages, by contrast, are contracts and there are legal provisions for terminating contracts when necessary. Every agreement can be superseded by another agreement. If there were no way out of a failed marriage, the couple's life would be torture. Family unity would be no better than slavery.

Spouses who cannot find solutions to their problems become desperate and may not see situations clearly. This is why Islam allows divorce, but in principle assigns the right of divorce to men, on the theory that they are likely to act more resolutely than women. However, if it has been previously stipulated in the marriage contract, there is no obstacle to giving the right of divorce to women as well. This is known in Islamic law as *tafwid al-talaq*. Even if the right of divorce has not been given to the wife in the marriage contract, under some circumstances she can still appeal to a court for divorce.

In order to avoid unnecessary divorce, men and women should appreciate each other's significance and respect each other. Memories, happy moments, welfare, tranquility and all the pleasurable things in life can be achieved under the shadow of divine wisdom. Success will manifest itself through mutual fidelity and sincerity. It is stated in the sayings of the Prophet (peace and blessings be upon him):

"When a man wakes up at night, wakens his wife and they pray two cycles of formal prayer together, they are recorded among the men and women who make much mention of Allah." (Abu Dawud, *Tatawwu'*, 18; *Witr*, 13)

"May Allah show mercy to a man who gets up during the night and prays, who wakens his wife and she prays; if she refuses, he sprinkles water on her face. May Allah show mercy to a woman who gets up during the night and prays, who wakens her husband and he prays; if he refuses she sprinkles water on his face." (Abu Dawud, *Tatawwu'*, 17; *Witr*, 12)

According to the aforementioned Prophetic sayings we can conclude that happiness in a family depends on two great principles:

1. Sincerity of the both parties

2. Mutual encouragement to piety.

Q - Considering all the things you have stated so far, is there any ideal, exemplary family you might point out to us?

Of the many examples that might be given, undoubtedly the family of Prophet Muhammad (peace and blessings be upon him) stands at the forefront.

Marriage and Family in Islam

As was true in every other aspect of life, the Prophet displayed the finest behavior in family life. He was the perfect husband and the best father. His blessed wife, our mother Khadija, was the most excellent example of a wife and mother. His other wives were good examples, too. No negative incidents can be found in his family life, although there were some small quarrels between his wives. Even those small incidents were solved and ended up well, thanks to the exemplary character of the Prophet and they set an example for the whole Muslim community.

Just as the personality of the Prophet was the best of personalities, his home was also the most ideal and exemplary home. His home was such a peaceful and tranquil place that even though his household might have no hot meal on the table for days, every visitor could feel its happiness. There was no trace of luxury: none of his wives had more than a modest room. Yet the most delicious meal for them all was contentedness, patience and submission. The method of discipline which the Messenger of Allah (peace and blessings be upon him) applied in his home filled the hearts of his household with endless love and loyalty. No woman can love her husband as much as the Prophet's wives loved him; no husband can love his wife as much as the Prophet loved his wives. No child can love its father as much as Fatima loved her father; and no father can love his children as much as the Prophet loved his.

The Messenger of Allah (peace and blessings be upon him) paid utmost attention to doing justice to all his wives. Even though he did his best in this regard, because of the difficulty of ensuring absolute justice, he prayed to Allah:

"Dear Lord! Unwittingly I may love one of them more than the others and that is inequity. Lord! I take refuge in Your mercy concerning this matter that I am incapable of preventing."[4]

Dear Lord! Bestow upon us and upon our families a pious life with which You are content. Make our homes a Paradise of felicity and blessings. Protect our homes from being a scene from Hell.

Amin!

---

4. There are many lessons behind the Prophet's confession of his weakness. One of them is to ensure that his followers do not forget that he was a human being, since some previous religious communities went so far in their respect to their prophets that they considered them to be gods. The same precaution explains why, in the second statement of the Islamic testimony of faith, the declaration that the Prophet is Allah's servant comes before the declaration that he is Allah's Messenger. Of course, considering him to be merely a servant and forgetting his prophethood is a great manifestation of ignorance!

Things that Women Need to Pay Attention to in the Family

"A pious woman makes her husband happy when he looks at her face; she fulfills her husband's licit requests; and when he is away from her, she protects his property and honor."

(Ibn Maja, *Nikah*, 5/1857)

Things that Women Need to Pay Attention

Q - What things do women need to pay attention to in order to protect their families' peace and happiness?

First of all, women need to be careful about their service to Allah and to be devout. In this respect they need to pay attention to their prayers and worship in addition to being sensitive about what is lawful and what is prohibited in Islam.

A woman's piety should manifest in her family through encouraging her husband, her children, her relatives and even her neighbors to give charity and perform good deeds. A pious woman is like a sweet-smelling flower of Paradise!

The most important task of a woman, after service to Allah, is to make her husband and her other family members happy. Making her husband happy and not shadowing the happiness of the family will grant a wife the contentment of Allah the Almighty. In fact the Prophet (peace and blessings be upon him) says in this regard:

A pious woman makes her husband happy when he looks at her face; she fulfills her husband's licit requests and when he is away from her, she protects his property and honor. (Ibn Maja, *Nikah*, 5/1857)

Therefore a pious woman looks for ways to make her family happy and she finds them.

> Q - Can we elaborate this matter a little more? To what things does a wife need to pay most attention in her daily life and in her house?

At home she must take great care of herself. She needs to be clean and well-groomed. Being untended and dirty will make her husband lose his respect for her. A wife should stay away from all appearances that her husband does not like, because if a man cannot find what he looks for in a woman in his wife, his heart may turn toward what is inappropriate and prohibited, which will destroy the happiness and peace in the family. So a wise woman offers herself like a bouquet of flowers to her grateful husband. It is in her best interests that he look forward to being at home in the evening.

A pious woman should meet her husband at the door with a smiling face and in the morning should send him off to work with kind words and prayers. Even if her own day's work has exhausted her, she should conceal her fatigue and not make a wry face in front of him. She should share her husband's worries and help him to relax.

She should keep the counsel of her own emotions rather than disturb the tranquility of the house. Umm Sulaym (may Allah be pleased with her), a Companion of the Prophet, gave an extraordinary example of such behavior. Even the death of her child did not overcome her compassion toward her husband. According to the narrative, Abu Talha's son, who had been gravely ill, died when his father was not home. Umm Sulaym washed and enshrouded the body. She commanded the other members of the household, "Do not tell Abu Talha of his son's death before I tell do." When Abu Talha came home, he asked, "How is my son?"

Umm Sulaym replied, "His pains are relieved and I think he is resting right now." Then she brought her husband dinner and after that they went to bed. In the morning, when Abu Talha wanted to go out, Umm Sulaym said, "Abu Talha! What do you think of what our neighbors did? I left something in their trust and they did not give it back when I asked for it."

Abu Talha said, "They did wrong."

Then Umm Sulaym said, "O Abu Talha! Your son was entrusted to you by Allah the Almighty. He has reclaimed His trust."

For a while Abu Talha was baffled and quiet. Then he said, *"We belong to Allah and to Allah we are continuously returning."*

When Abu Talha went to the mosque for prayer, he told everything to the Messenger of Allah (peace and blessings be upon him). The Prophet prayed for them, "O Allah! Bestow your blessing upon them with regard to that night of theirs."

Less than a year later, Allah granted the couple another son. The Messenger of Allah took a date, chewed it, took some of it out of his mouth, put it into the child's mouth and named him Abdullah – "Servant of Allah." It is narrated that seven out of Abdullah's nine children memorized the whole Qur'an as a result of the blessings of the aforementioned prayer. (Bukhari, *Jana'iz*, 42: *Aqiqa*, 1; Muslim, *Adab*, 23: *Fada'il al-Sahaba*, 107)

> *Q - What other things does a wife need to be careful about in her relations with her husband?*

She should never neglect her husband and never put him in second place among the members of the family. A normal man cannot accept to be in second place, for that is against his nature.

In order to please someone, we need to know that person well. This is why a woman should try to understand her husband and learn his values, inter-

Things that Women Need to Pay Attention

ests and feelings. Naturally a man should treat his wife in the same way. If both of them do not pay attention to this necessary work of relationship, then *"unity, sharing and things in common,"* the natural requirements of a successful marriage, fade over time and spouses move away from each other emotionally. If timely precautions are not taken, the situation can become so serious that the original love and affection between spouses may give way to hatred and separation. The worst season for this danger is the time of old age. The inward isolation of spouses who did not try to get to know each other over all those years turns into a desperate loneliness, an irreversible point of regret and longing.

A wife should help her husband in all of his good and lawful deeds. She should show respect to his relatives. If she has to make a choice or sacrifice, she should show the greater attention to her husband's family.

Life is full of surprises. There are times of crisis and grief. A wife should stay next to her husband during these times and help him with his burden. How nicely our predecessors expressed this: *"Be like a rug and let forty feet walk on you, so that you become the crown on their heads."* What we understand from this and similar proverbs is that being able to conceal our pains during times of crisis is a virtue. The Prophet never forgot his wife Khadija's strong support, patience, understanding, submission and sacrifices.

A wife enters her home in her wedding dress, fill it with joy and happiness and leaves it, when she starts her eternal life, in her white burial shroud. All people should love in order to be loved, show respect in order to be respected, make sacrifices in order to be blessed. However all these should first come from the wife in a family. An intelligent woman knows how to please her husband and build happiness in the family. In a hadith, it is stated:

When a wife whose husband is content with her dies, she enters Paradise. (Tirmidhi, *Rada*, 10; See also, Ibn Maja, *Nikah*, 4)

This tradition expresses not only the great reward awaiting a pious wife who pleases her husband, but also the place of the husband in the family and the deep spiritual value of the manners of a wife. Husbands, on their part, are expected to be sensitive about how and where they earn their family's livelihood and try their best to refrain from income from obscure sources that may possibly be unethical or illicit. For as the Prophetic tradition about choosing a marriage partner says, ""*People's rank is hidden in their religion; their dignity is hidden in their reason; and the beauty of their progeny is hidden in the goodness of their morality [protected by marriage].*"

A pious woman not only loves her husband but also shows a reasonable level of respect to his relatives and friends. Such behavior would certainly please her husband, too. However, there is an important point

Things that Women Need to Pay Attention

involved here: we must not forget the borders of lawfulness drawn by Islam. When a woman is alone at home, she cannot invite inside men who, if she were single, she would legally be permitted to marry. This is a very sensitive issue. Nobody can protest good will while breaking the limits of Islamic law. A woman in particular must take great care to stay away from anything that might blemish her name. For in our society, a woman's honor is like a white dress: even the tiniest stain offends the eyes. The Messenger of Allah (peace and blessings be upon him) warned his followers about "grey areas": *"Stay away from doubtful places."*

One night when the Prophet (peace and blessings be upon him) was walking with one of his wives on the street, two men from Medina saw them. The Prophet (peace and blessings be upon him) immediately informed them, *"She is (my wife) Safiyya daughter of Huyyay."*

Both of them said, "O Messenger, hallowed be Allah! [We cannot conceive of anything suspicious about you even in the remotest corners of our minds.]" He replied,

Satan circulates in the human body like the blood in our veins and I was afraid lest it should instill some evil in your heart. (Bukhari, *I'tikaf*, 11; Muslim, *Kitab al-Salam*, 23-25)

Thus our Master's example advises his followers not to do anything that might remotely produce doubt or suspicion in others.

A wife should always be next to her husband and support his good deeds so that he may find consolation with her and eagerly carry out his plans. It is well known that sharing increases our happiness and decreases our sorrow. Spouses should never forget that they are each other's companions not just in the journey of this world but also in the journey of the Hereafter. Though they had separate lives before, through marriage their two lives have become one. Therefore they should observe the principles of unity in all aspects of life. If one of them slips, the other spouse should help him (or her) to stand up.

A wife should watch her husband's mood. When she feels that her husband is upset by some small thing, she should not exaggerate the issue and turn into a debate. Longer and more serious disputes may run the risk of damaging mutual love and respect. Even in such cases, it is better for the lady of the house to be gentle and to maintain her calm. Eventually her husband will realize his fault, come to his senses and show respect to his wife. If she presses the argument, he may grow stubborn and become unable to see his fault at all. Then Satan will enter between them and sow the seeds of hatred and enmity in their hearts.

Another significant matter which spouses should be careful about is jealousy. One of the most disturbing issues in a relationship is distrust. Even when there is some real cause for suspicion, spouses should try to sit and talk rather than blaming each other. Otherwise small issues may easily turn into big conflicts.

Sometimes people are not able to see the results of their actions in difficult situations. They may forget, or make mistakes. If a woman finds her husband in need of her opinion, she should sincerely and diligently make him feel that she supports him. Then she should tell him what she thinks is the best solution to the problem...for a wife should also be her husband's most intimate friend. We should never forget that man and woman complete each other.

From time to time the Mothers of the Believers, the wives of the Messenger of Allah (peace and blessings be upon him), supported him with their ideas. For instance, during the negotiation of the treaty of Hudaybiyya, many Companions of the Prophet were deeply discontented with the treaty's terms and grew restive. They could not comprehend the wisdom behind the treaty and were hoping it would be annulled. Most of them wanted to fight. This made the Prophet extremely sad. His wife Umm Salama (may Allah be pleased with her) counseled him not to worry, but immediately to perform the personal obligation required by the treaty. She knew that there was a possibility that the Hudaybiyya negotiations might fail unless the Prophet himself applied the treaty's conditions. As a result of Umm Salama's advice, the

Messenger of Allah cut his hair and took off his *ihram*, publicly terminating his intention for Pilgrimage, which was what the treaty required. Seeing him do this, the Companions followed his lead. Thus the problem was solved before it was too late.

Another example is displayed by our mother Khadija. She consoled the Prophet (peace and blessings be upon him) after the first revelation, when he was frightened and worried about his mission. And she was the one who suggested that the Prophet seek out and consult the monk Waraqa b. Nawfal so that he might be reassured about his calling.

Even Caliph 'Umar (may Allah be pleased with him) once listened to a woman's counsel. One day in the mosque he was complaining that women were requesting extortionate amounts of dowry, which made marriage very difficult. He declared that he intended to set a limit on dowry requests. A woman from the back rows stood up and objected. She quoted from the Qur'an (4:20) that women could specify whatever amount of dowry they might wish. Hearing this, 'Umar understood his fault and changed his opinion saying,

"She is right. 'Umar has made a mistake." ('Ali al-Muttaqi, XVI, 536-537/45796)

However, there is a delicate point here that needs mentioning. When a wife is asked for her opinion, she should be careful not to seem arrogant, even though her opinion is correct. Whenever she is giv-

Things that Women Need to Pay Attention

ing advice to her husband, she should avoid appearing disrespectful toward her husband. It is a fact that men often feel uncomfortable when they are advised by women. In short, a righteous woman knows how to use her intelligence in the matter of her relations with her husband.

A woman should have the skill and mastery to enter her husband's heart. There are many examples of this in our history. Many of the Ottoman sultans' wives shared the power of their husbands through winning their husbands' hearts. By doing so, they were able to leave many religious charitable foundations and good deeds behind them. Because of their services, they are still remembered with blessings and gratitude.

It is not appropriate for a wife to criticize or correct her husband in front of other people. No matter how wrong he is, she should not embarrass him by revealing his faults. The principle holds just as well for husbands' treatment of their wives. In a verse, it is stated that

… Your wives are a garment for you and you are a garment for them …" (2; 187)

It is also wrong for a wife to praise other men above her husband. She should not complain about her husband even to her parents, as well as being careful not to put him in difficult positions in front of other people. She should look for ways to solve their problems between them.

We observe, in our experience, that at the foundation of a couple's unhappiness one usually finds a failure to appreciate each other. Spouses can be each other's Paradise or each other's Hell. When a pious woman pays attention both to serving Allah and to responding to her husband's lawful requests, it is a sign that she is on the path to Heaven.

> *Q - What kinds of good news have been given by the Prophet (peace and blessings be upon him) about such righteous women?*

The Prophet (peace and blessings be upon him) says:

After mindfulness of Allah, a believer gains nothing better for himself than a pious wife who obeys him when he commands her and pleases him when he looks at her. When he asks her to carry out a task, she is true to him and when he is away she protects her chastity as well as her husband's property." (Ibn Maja, *Nikah*, 5/1857)

A good wife is the one who obeys her husband and is compassionate to her children.

"The whole world is providence and the best provision of the world is a pious woman." (Muslim, *Kitab al-Rada*, 64; See also: Nasa`i, *Nikah*, 15; Ibn Maja, *Nikah*, 5)

Thawban (may Allah be pleased with him) narrates:

Things that Women Need to Pay Attention

When the verse *"...and (as for) those who hoard up gold and silver and do not spend it in Allah's way, announce to them a painful chastisement"* (9:34) was revealed, we were with the Prophet (peace and blessings be upon him) on an expedition. Some of the Companions said that now that we knew the ruling about gold and silver [we would no longer hoard them, but give them in charity]. We wished we knew what is good for us, so that we could accumulate that instead. Upon hearing this, the Messenger of Allah said, *"The most valuable possessions are a tongue that mentions the names of Allah, a thankful heart and a wife who strengthens the faith of her husband."* (Tirmidhi, *Tafsir*, 9/9)

> *Q - People experience so many financial difficulties in the contemporary world. With regard to our property, what principles might we observe in order to save the peace and tranquility of our families?*

First of all, people need to learn how to control their desires so that they can prevent themselves from buying everything they see. Otherwise, constant expenditures will put them under a heavy financial burden and that will lead to unrest and crisis at home. Today many families, because of the ever-increasing credit cards, believe that they should easily be able to own whatever they want. In this way they fall into deep whirlpools of debt and interest. Many happy families have been destroyed by falling into this trap. Even if spouses are rich, they should not waste their wealth. This is an obligation for both man and woman. It is as Allah the Almighty commands in the following a verse:

And give to the near of kin his due and (to) the needy and the wayfarer and do not squander wastefully. Surely the squanderers are the fellows of the devils and the Devil is ever ungrateful to his Lord. (17:26-27)

If anyone owns more than he or she needs, then he or she should look for needy people to help. Helping the poor and attaining their prayers cheers up homes and increases our blessings. It should always be kept in mind that we could be in their place and they could be in our place.

Our principle in charity should be the verse *"By no means shall you attain to righteousness until you spend (benevolently) out of what you love; …"* (3:92). When we give in charity, we should not give from the worst things that we own, but from the things that we value. In a saying of the Prophet (peace and blessings be upon him) it is metaphorically stated that *"Those who give charity first give it into the hand of Allah; and from the hand of Allah, it transfers to the hands of the poor."*

It should especially be mentioned that in families, practicing frugality is primarily the duty of the wife. She should be modest in her spending and

Things that Women Need to Pay Attention

careful about avoiding extravagance. If she does this, her home will be a prosperous one even if its people are not rich. In order to achieve this prosperity, she should begin cooking with the name of Allah, use her ingredients wisely and not push the financial limits of the family. This is the basis of domestic happiness. Today, because we do not observe these principles and because we throw tons of food into trash bins, we do not have prosperity and blessing in our homes. Meanwhile, a pious Muslim woman will prevent waste by buying just enough provisions for her home.

In times gone by, women were very skilled in patching clothes and never discarded anything until it was worn out. Today, however, many women prefer to discard their clothes and buy new ones when there are even the tiniest tears. This is a terribly extravagant practice.

The last thing that I would like to emphasize concerning the role of women in a peaceful family environment is the reality of the old saying, "A female bird makes the nest." When wives grasp the significance of this saying and perform their duties in that spirit, our homes become gardens of Paradise. The responsibility then falls to husbands to appreciate and protect the environment their wives have created.

Things That Men Need to Pay Attention to in the Family

Supporting the religious and moral growth of women and children, assisting their education in the ways that will bring them eternal happiness, are among the most significant duties of men.

Things That Men Need to Pay Attention

Q – What things does a man most need to pay attention to in his family?

The happiness of a family depends on a righteous father's strength of will. To be a righteous father means to be a father who provides his family with sustenance, discipline and protection. All these require a man to be intelligent, experienced, skilled and especially to have strong faith and good morals.

Q - Could we clarify this point with more details? What does a father have to provide for his family?

When a man decides to marry, before everything else he needs a lawful source of income in order to support his family in an ethical fashion, since Islam assigns the responsibility of providing a family's sustenance to the father. (It is because of this responsibility that the Qur'anic laws of inheritance allow men to inherit larger shares than women.) Only when a man has the means to support his prospective family may he take the rest of the steps necessary to get married. Marriage is simply not appropriate for a man who cannot even support himself, let alone a whole household. On the other hand, if those who are not financially very strong hope to get married in order to better their practice of Islam, then Allah will surely help them. As the verse says:

And marry those among you who are single and those who are fit among your male slaves and your female slaves; if they are needy, Allah will make them free from want out of His grace; and Allah is Ample-giving, Knowing. (24:32)

As may be understood from this verse, those who have financial means enough to get married should marry and those who do not have the means should be helped to get married. This is the responsibility of a Muslim society. Such help is a perfect opportunity to gain spiritual rewards. In that way, the chastity of society and of individuals are both protected.

Chastity is a distinctive virtue, given to human beings alone. Chastity cannot even be considered for other creatures. However, if humans lose this quality, they descend to the level of the other animals.

Undoubtedly, intelligence, strength, capabilities, qualities and inclinations are created in each person in varying measure. Because of different temperaments, different occupations have emerged. All these occupations and professions are needed for the continuance of the social order. Society as a whole needs

Things That Men Need to Pay Attention

and will always have butchers, street cleaners, doctors, scholars, and many other functions and roles. This being the case, everybody should try to get married according to his means and the prospective husband should seek a socially compatible wife.

For a husband and a wife to have similar financial status is certainly important, but there are other matters of interest, too. Similar knowledge, manners and customs are also important. If this sort of resemblance can be achieved, the family will be free of disputes rooted in differences of social status. For instance, if a man cannot provide the standard of living that his wife is accustomed to, the resulting embarrassment and discontent might well cause the destruction of their family. Mutual love can sometimes prevent this, but it is rare. Therefore marriages between members of families from similar social levels are usually the right choice and more beneficial. All these means is that people who share world views, spiritual values, goals and wishes can get along with each other more easily.

In any case, family expenses and lifestyle must be regulated according to the father's level of income. It is not right for a mother and her children to ask more from a man than he earns. But the father is fully responsible to provide their *"housing, food and clothes"* to the extent of his income.

Housing, be it rented or owned, must be big enough for the size of the family and should be located in a good neighborhood. To persist in living in a bad, unhealthy neighborhood when there is enough financial means to move elsewhere, is unfair to the members of the family. This mistake can eventually result in the moral decline and destruction of the family.

Meals should also be regulated according to the income level of the father. In pursuit of subsistence, fathers should neither show laziness nor force themselves to work beyond their physical strength. A husband's responsibility is to provide food within the limits of this balance. The same balance must be observed in other expenditures, too.

Both extravagance and stinginess should be avoided. Unfortunately extravagance is one of the greatest problems of our world today. Many people are neglectful when it comes to wasting resources. The habit has become widespread – yet men should protect themselves from unnecessary expenditures even if they are wealthy. Otherwise they will eventually be crushed under the heavy burden of extravagance.

Eating at least enough to live is obligatory; eating as much as needed is permitted; but eating more than that is not allowed. The Sufis have looked at the habits of eating like this:

"According to the law of Sharia, to keep eating after you are full is extravagance.

Things That Men Need to Pay Attention

According to the path of the Sufis, to keep eating until you are full is extravagance."

Fathers should be sensitive and alert about the fruits and vegetables that their children like. Children who are not able to ask for what they want because of shyness, especially girls, must be given special care.

Guests require generous service as Islamic hospitality advises. This is both a moral virtue and one of the honors of being human.

The father of the house must provide at least two sets of clothes, one for winter and the other for summer, for every member of the family. There is nothing wrong with having an extra suit for special occasions. Islam encourages us to beautify ourselves within certain limits; however wearing clothes that are too showy and bragging about it, or looking down on people, are prohibited by Islam.

Silk clothes and accessories made of gold, like rings or watches, are prohibited for men. These materials are for women's use and their usage by men leads to moral degeneration. This principle must be observed in choosing clothes and accessories for boys. Letting our daughters wear revealing clothes or boys' clothes, relying on the excuse of "letting her satisfy her childhood desires," is a great mistake. In time, such clothes will turn into a habit and getting rid of that habit will not be easy. Ultimately, the child's future may be lost. Therefore, girls must become accustomed to an Islamic standard of dressing and taught its significance. Otherwise, there is always the danger that early wrong directions and mistaken actions will damage our daughters' dignity as grown women. Let us particularly remember that observing Islamic standards of dress is not just a way of protecting our daughters, but also a means of fostering splendor and grace among Muslim women. Women who dress according to Islamic principles will always be manifestations of dignity and virtue. Such a presence evokes only feelings of respect in the hearts of others.

Q – What is a man's responsibility towards his family's moral education?

To support the religious and moral growth of women and children, assisting their education in the ways that will bring them eternal happiness, are among the most significant duties of men. The Qur'an states:

O you who believe! Save yourselves and your families from a fire whose fuel is men and stones ... (66:6)

The full scope of this task encompasses the members of our families, our relatives, our neighbors and ultimately everybody in the country according to their positions and potentials; because just as families shape their greater environment, so also does the greater environment shape our families.

Things That Men Need to Pay Attention

A father should pay attention to his family's Qur'anic education and inspire them with a love for worshipping Allah. At the same time, it is necessary for him to teach his family the manners and customs of society. To address both needs, when children reach at the age of primary school, it is wise for a father to send them to summer schools for learning Qur'an. Later, when they graduate from primary school, full-time Qur'anic school is an excellent idea. This is important especially for girls. We should never forget that the most valuable legacy that parents can leave for their children is a happy life in the Hereafter. How happy are those who help their children to memorize the entire Qur'an and adorn them with the beauties of the Qur'an! According to a hadith:

If anyone recites the Qur'an and acts according to its teachings, on the Day of Judgment his parents will be crowned with a crown whose light, if it were among you, would be better than the light of the sun in all the dwellings of this world. So imagine the light of the person who acts according to the teachings! (Abu Dawud, *Witr*, 14).

Today people make great efforts and pay great amounts of money to learn foreign languages and draw comparisons among colleges based on their success in teaching languages. On the other hand we have come to ignore and even belittle, our Qur'anic schools. Yet leaving our children deprived of the spirit of the Qur'an is a very sad situation. And we forget that the greatest success, which may well save our lives in the Hereafter, is to be able to leave behind good children, who will pray for us.

Our children should be raised aware of the Qur'anic spirit and its blessings. They should particularly be taught the parables of the prophets in the Qur'an and their messages. In the contemporary world, supporting our children's faith is a necessity if we are to protect them from the dangers of atheism. Besides offering them Qur'anic education, we should also teach our children the life and Sunna of the Prophet (peace and blessings be upon him), since he is the living interpretation of the Qur'an. In order to properly learn the meaning of his life and to harmonize with it, we need to follow in his footsteps and try to be like him.

If parents neglect their tasks and do not give their children proper religious education, those children will grow up under the influence of the media and the materialistic life styles they promote. Television will turn into their mother. It will feed them, condition their imagination and thinking and even shape their physical appearance. Once this state of affairs takes hold, there is only one job left for parents to do and that is to fulfill their children's requests.

It is even more unfortunate for parents when children fall into the traps of immoral websites and TV programs. Ignoring them is a signal for the punishment of the parents. The simplest illustration of the danger is that today's children know the names and lives of many sports figures and celebrities and try to be like them. Yet they do not even know the names of their own prophets, let alone their exemplary lives! This means that the children are actually being raised by football players and movie stars. Parents now get the trouble of feeding their children's physical bodies, but the children's spirits are fed by strangers. How long can a society and a culture survive under these conditions? If we are to succeed in the battle of cultures, we must be very careful about our children's education. We must educate them according to Islamic principles. Our children must grow up from their own roots.

Islam promotes certain standards of dress; they are proper to human dignity. One of them is the prohibition of wearing tight and transparent clothes that reveal the body. When the Messenger of Allah (peace and blessings be upon him) saw Aisha's sister Asma' wearing a transparent dress, he turned his head away.

He said, "O Asma', once a woman reaches puberty, it does not suit her to display any of the parts of her body except this and this," and he pointed to her face and hands. (Abu Dawud, *Libas*, 31)

These are basic Islamic principles formulated to prevent behavior which is not appropriate to human dignity. Men and women must act together to observe these principles.

Even before children reach the age of puberty, parents must separate the rooms of their daughters and their sons. This is something that needs to be done in order to mature them spiritually and shape their personalities.

Q - What are the responsibilities of men for the protection of their families?

A man has to protect his family from all kinds of negative influences. A father should keep children away from friends and places that may spoil their religion and morality, from the immoral shows on television, from vicious and worthless books and magazines. In short, protecting the family from attacks arriving both inside and outside the home is the responsibility of men.

Q - Is there anything else which men should be particularly careful about in the guidance of their families?

Men should observe the religious limits. Unless it is absolutely necessary, they should stay away from places where men and women work together. If a man has to work in such a place, he should control his eyes and his acts; he should always observe the manners of our religion. If he is an employer, he should arrange the working hours and workplaces of male and female employees so as to eliminate the

Things That Men Need to Pay Attention

necessity of working in a mixed environment. If he needs to work privately with someone, staying alone together far from the eyes of others, he must choose that person from among his male employees. Such a condition is called *khalwat al-sahiha*, "true seclusion," which is forbidden between unrelated men and women according to Islamic law. Because of the risk of true seclusion, a male employer should not seek to employ female secretaries, whatever the excuse. Unfortunately, today many families are destroyed just because these principles are not followed.

A wise man leaves his business life out of his home. He does not bring his problems home.

An intelligent and insightful man forgives his family members' worldly mistakes and approaches them with mercy and compassion. He keeps his wife's secrets and deficiencies from everybody.

However, he does not ignore his family's faults in religious matters. He seriously confronts errors when they occur and heads off in advance mistakes that might be committed because of laziness or ignorance. He meticulously does everything possible to support the religious education of his family. He teaches his children himself as much as he can and when necessary, he also gets professional help from effective scholars. These things, too, are among the responsibilities of the father.

A husband should speak pleasantly and gently with his wife; he should not alienate her by approaching her rudely and harshly. The Messenger of Allah (peace and blessings be upon him) says:

The best of you is the one who is best in his treatment of women. (Tirmidhi, *Rada*, 11. See also Abu Dawud, *Sunna*, 15; Ibn Maja, *Nikah*, 50)

A man should consult with his wife in family matters and should not give her responsibilities heavier than she can handle. He should help his wife with child care and discipline, because both child care and housework may exhaust her. Helping women in their work will increase mutual love and strengthen family ties.

A husband should pray for the welfare of his wife. He should not go on long trips without telling her in advance. He should also not bring guests home without getting her consent first. He should never insist that his wife go out in front of strangers to serve them. He should keep his family away from mixed environments as much as possible.

Q - If men follow the aforementioned principles and properly perform their responsibilities, what rewards do they receive?

In a sense, Islam entrusts the family to the father. Our tradition assigns him both particular rights and also the particular responsibility of providing for all his family's material and spiritual needs. That is the meaning of the leadership position is given to a father.

A father is like the sun in the sky of a family; a mother is like the moon, covered with veils of chastity; and the children are like the stars.

A father who devotes his entire energy, power and intelligence to his family's welfare, discipline and education of course deserves to be respected, loved and obeyed. It is a great mistake to rebel against, disobey, or talk disgracefully to such a father. This is why the Prophet (peace and blessings be upon him) says:

Allah's pleasure is hidden in a father's contentment and Allah's anger is hidden in a father's anger. (Tirmidhi, *Birr*, 3)

Mother and children alike need to obey and respect the father, who is the leader of the family. A father's significance can be felt especially when he is gone. This is why family members should know a father's value before it is too late and try to get his good prayers while he is alive. They should follow his lawful orders and should not fail in respect for him.

Things that Men and Women Together Need to Pay Attention to in the Family

The most compassionate parents are those who prepare each other and their children to be servants of Allah the Almighty.

Things that Men and Women Need to Pay Attention

Q - A man and a woman build a home and decide to share everything. What are the primary matters they need to attend to together?

We should always remember that there are two great undertakings of life in common that have equal significance: sharing happiness and joy and sharing problems and burdens. Ideally, sharing is comprehensive, embracing every aspect of life, both spiritual and material. It may seem easier to share happiness, but sorrow and troubles also need to be shared. Husbands and wives should support each other under every circumstance: they should be like two hands washing each other. Life cannot always be perfect. We should not forget that there are ups and downs, storms, twists and accidents in life. Life is full of unknowns and surprises and destiny is a divine secret. This is why the greatest support for a believer is his or her faith in Allah and submission to Allah's will. The second biggest support comes from a loving spouse. It should not be forgotten that when desperate and helpless people do not find the support they need from their families, they are often dragged into bigger problems. On the other hand, if a person in trouble has a spiritually mature and understanding family, any problem can be handled.

The soundness of a family depends on the spiritual maturity and mutual understanding of its members. This is the most significant requirement for attaining good results from a marriage. Mawlana Jalaluddin Rumi's famous words allude to this reality:

Listen to this truth from the rose, hear what it says: "Why should I feel sad, why should I bemoan my life among thorns? I won my ability to smile by keeping company with prickliness and through enduring that, I grew able to disperse beauty and emit perfume to the world."

This rose is telling us, "Be like me!"

Q - What do we need to do in order to establish a sound family structure?

First of all, happiness in a family can only be achieved mutually. The foundations of mutual happiness are:

1. Treat each other kindly;
2. Behave thoughtfully and maturely;
3. Put the other person first.

These habits can easily be attained by people who pursue morality, intelligence, wisdom, sincerity and mutual sensitivity as personal goals.

Things that Men and Women Need to Pay Attention

In order to get along with each other, spouses need five great qualities: piety, virtue, love, compassion and fidelity. The importance of these qualities is very obvious in our society now, since we hear of so many tragedies emerging every day due to the lack of them.

Piety and virtue are the basis of all other good qualities in a family, just as they are in a society. Homes where members live according to Islamic principles bestow upon themselves and upon their societies the happiness of both worlds. But when members of a family move away from Islam, not only the other family members but also the entire society is negatively affected.

We do need to properly understand piety. A person cannot be both pious and rude at the same time. Islam is entirely composed of courtesy and grace. As it is stated by a poet:

Manners are a crown made from the light of the Lord

To be safe from all calamities, put on that crown

Rumi says:

My intelligence bent down to my ear and asked, "What is religion?"

My heart replied, "Religion is good manners."

The next great necessity, love, is the power connecting family members to each other and strengthening their ties. When love decreases, the foundations of a family start to collapse. Love has to be mutual. A man will be loved by his family exactly as much as he loves them. And love is not just a feeling, it is an attitude: the more love increases, the more hearts should be adorned by grace, courtesy and respect. Love should not turn into thoughtless levity and certain manners should always be observed. Love, mercy and other similar emotions must be temperately expressed. Excessive love can damage a relationship. Complete lack of love, however, may lead those left hungry for it to search for it in bad places. While excessive, selfish love will lead to overmastering possessiveness and jealousy, lack of love can lead to lack of any care at all about the spouse's behavior. Both of these are disasters for a family.

One needs to be equally careful about excess and deficiency of compassion. Too much mercy can lead to supineness; it may end in the toleration of disastrous mistakes. This is not mercy, but weakness of heart. Lack of compassion, on the other hand, hardens the heart and leads a person to oppression and violence. Moderation in compassion gives good results and brings happiness to a family. The most compassionate parents are those who can wake up their children for dawn prayer, thus preparing them for eternal happiness.

As for fidelity, it is one of the most important matters. Both parties must be careful to take it seriously. Fidelity means to be honest and faithful in every aspect of life. Of course, each partner's avoidance of words and actions that might damage the other's confidence is very important for the continuity of their marriage. It is also very important for partners to value their faithfulness to each other, so that they vigilantly protect their eyes and hearts from slipping to outsiders. Spouses should meticulously observe Islamic principles governing the interactions of men and women in order to avoid falling into undesirable situations. Actions and behaviors that run the risk of provoking suspicion, gossip and doubts both damage a person's honor and reputation among people and endanger a family's future.

Another manifestation of fidelity and loyalty is to respect and serve the parents of one's spouse. Both bride and groom should accustom themselves to treating their fathers-in-law and mothers-in-law like their own parents. They will soon enough find themselves in the same position, when their own children get married! If they injure their in-laws, they may very well face similar injury in the future.

> *Q - You have mentioned that it is a man's task to provide the sustenance of his family. Does this responsibility necessitate economy?*

As we have mentioned before, providing for a family's needs is the responsibility of men. However, this does not mean that men must immediately

A Peaceful Home

provide everything a family member might desire. Lawful and necessary demands should be responded to according to the family's financial means. When someone's every request is instantly fulfilled, it leads to spoiling and spoiling can lead to depravity and rebellion. In time, such a person will start thinking only of his or her private benefit. He or she will come to treat other family members like servants. This is why a believer should control his or her desires, even when the necessary financial means are available. The moderation of desires is a very important discipline, indispensible if we are to reach spiritual maturity and attain Allah's pleasure. Patience is more important when we have the means than when we do not, because wealth continuously provokes selfishness.

Divine wisdom provides us with an educational method that will help us to control our desires and to spiritually mature. Allah the Almighty sometimes refuses His servants' supplications and wishes, sometimes accepts them and sometimes postpones them. The object is to remind us servants not to attach ourselves to the temporal world and to help us realize that we are always in need of Allah's assistance. Humans hate leaving this world even when we live under severe conditions of poverty and want. Should we be capable of fulfilling every whim, we would never want to leave, or ever think about the Hereafter! Such heedlessness drags people into ever-greater mistakes and even into rebellion against Allah the Almighty.

Adam (peace and blessings be upon him) made the mistake of not wanting to leave Paradise and, as a result, he was expelled from it. Therefore when our children want something from us, we need to take into consideration not just the possible problems it may cause them in this world, but also what the effects may be for them on Judgment Day.

Of course, restricting expenditures too much, to the level of stinginess and refusing to provide even vital necessities can never be acceptable behavior. An intelligent person follows a balanced path between the two extremes. The Qur'an commends:

… those who, when they spend, are neither extravagant nor parsimonious and (keep) between these the just mean. (25:67)

The middle path is the balance of life. Stinginess is abominable. Extravagance too is an unacceptable quality for a Muslim. Even a wealthy Muslim is not allowed to waste his or her wealth. Nobody has the right to say, "This is my property and I can do with it whatever I want." Wealth belongs to Allah the Almighty. He has only entrusted it to people in this world. On the Day of Judgment, He will question us about where and how we spent our wealth. This is expressed in the following verse:

And give to the near of kin his due and (to) the needy and the wayfarer and do not squander wastefully. Surely the squanderers are the fellows of the devils and the devil is ever ungrateful to his Lord. (17:26-27)

Islam prohibits all kinds of extravagance for everybody. It does not matter whether the person it waylays is the family's father or mother: extravagance in a family is a disease to be prevented. When this disease penetrates into a person's soul, it is really difficult for that person to live in peace.

Today the disease we call "spending madness" drags many people into dissatisfaction with what they have and makes them treat abnormal expenditures as normal. Constantly changing furniture, appliances, cell phones, cars and other possessions, even though they are in no need of change; buying new clothes merely to follow new fashions; and insisting on buying only certain pricey brands are all destructive effects of this disease. The result of all this futile expense is nothing other than disappointment and frustration. Those who try to cover their costs with credit cards, submitting themselves to usurious transactions, are doomed to be devastated when their financial means fall short. Finally the victims of this disease will attempt to blame people around them for not helping out. All this is the result of not using reason and emotion together, in a balanced fashion.

Allah created poverty and wealth to test people's gratitude and patience. Therefore we should turn to the blessing of patience in order to avoid contracting spending madness. A believer should consider that lack of means can help a servant to come closer to his Lord. Meanwhile, even the wealthiest and most heedless person in the world will remember Allah

Things that Men and Women Need to Pay Attention

and ask His help when in danger. It is when we human beings feel our weakness that we recognize ourselves. The messenger of Allah (peace and blessings be upon him) expressed his own weakness like this:

Dear Lord! I cannot properly know You. I cannot properly serve You.

Friends of Allah have suggested guidelines for dress that are in accord with the varying spiritual states of human beings.

At the level of Sharia, attire must fall within the limits of the permitted and the forbidden.

At the level of the tariqah, attire should be governed by necessity.

At the level of *Haqiqa*, concern with dress and appearance is inconceivable.

The best principle is to wear clean and simple clothes and then not let the matter occupy one's heart.

Islam has produced principles to help us understand not only how to earn wealth, but also how to spend it. If we cannot find anything productive to do with our money at home and as a result begin to waste it on pointless indulgences, we should remember the unfortunate people in the world and think about helping them. If we have already been helping them, then it is time to increase the amount of support. Those who are aware that the poor have rights over their wealth cannot spend it extravagantly. The Qur'an teaches:

And spend in the way of Allah and cast not yourselves to perdition with your own hands and do good (to others); surely Allah loves the doers of good. (2:195)

It should not be forgotten that there will be serious questioning in the next world for every single penny wasted. Meanwhile, in this world, there are many impoverished people who are struggling to survive.

All believers should reflect upon the many gifts Allah has bestowed upon us and be thankful for them all. We should recall that we are sleeping with full stomachs, while so many people in the world are hungry and thirsty. We are safe and secure, while so many people live in danger. We are sheltered in warm houses, while there are people freezing in the world. These are great blessings of Allah the Almighty; however they also place heavy responsibilities upon the shoulders of the believers.

This sort of reflection must be a well-established feature of our lives. As a matter of fact, Caliph 'Umar (may Allah be pleased with him), who is reported to have said, *"Question yourselves before you come to be questioned,"* used to reflect upon his responsibilities every night. He said, *"If, during my government, a sheep were to fall into the Tigris and drown, I am afraid that Allah the Almighty will hold me account-*

able for it on the Day of Judgment." He regularly asked himself, *"O 'Umar! What did you do today for Allah's sake?"*

We should ask ourselves how many times we have felt such emotions. On how many nights, after a long work day, have we questioned our hearts in such contemplation? Those who achieve this level of reflection attain a new characteristic that gives them spiritual peace and tranquility. It is contentment.

Contentment is the greatest wealth in the world. A person's level of spiritual wealth can be measured by his level of contentment. Contented people know how to be satisfied what they have. They are not greedy to get more. This leads them to accept their situation in life and eases their minds about it. However, contentment should never be misunderstood as laziness and the abandonment of working for a living! On the contrary, contentment with Allah's blessings only begins to take effect after we have committed ourselves to working within lawful limits. Those who are satisfied with what they have also strive to help others. Those who are not contented always more and instead of helping others, continually demand help for themselves.

We call the Prophetic era the Age of Happiness (*'asr al-sa'ada*). The community of those days was one in which all these and many other merits were manifested. It was a community that attained the furthest horizons of *wusla* – spiritual union. It was blessed time of knowing Allah and His Messenger (peace and blessings be upon him) intimately. In that community, people took worldly expectations and benefits out of their hearts. They viewed their property and their lives alike as means of coming closer to Allah and His Messenger. Faith was a pleasure and mercy was endless. Serving the creation of Allah the Almighty was way of life. To imitate what the Messenger of Allah did was the greatest ideal of the Companions. All of the counsels and warnings of the Prophet were accepted as sacred orders and observed meticulously.

The whole society of that time lived in contentment. Extravagance, luxury, excessive spending, greed and ostentation were qualities that the Companions did not know. They were aware of the fact that, as the saying goes, "tomorrow, the grave will be the residence of our souls." They placed Allah and His Messenger at the center of all their social relations. Although they had once been an ignorant community, after they were admitted to the school of faith, they achieved one of the greatest civilizations of history. Their hearts lived with the constant questions: "What does Allah require of me? What might the Messenger of Allah like to see from me?" For them, all of life was connected to Allah's pleasure. Among them, mercy and compassion deepened and sensitivity toward observing the rights of others and doing justice, reached its apex. For the Companions, the most joyful moments of life were the times when they conveyed the message of Allah to others.

Today, we should seek to follow in the footsteps of the Companions in order to reach the same spiritual levels they reached and to live in a peaceful and tranquil society, as they did. Mothers and fathers should seek to embody these beauties and to raise their children according to these principles.

It is particularly important that parents always treat their children equally and observe justice between them. People may not be able to control their inner feelings, but at least the outward expression of those feelings ought not to produce inequality among children. For instance, when something is purchased for one child, the same thing, or something similar, needs to be bought for the others. When one of them is kissed, the others should not be neglected. In short, parents should never allow jealousy to take root among their children.

People also need to search out residences in good neighborhoods and to be careful in their relationships with neighbors and relatives who show weakness in morality and religion. They should never put their own children in danger while hoping to correct other people's faults.

About Child Discipline

If we want perfect children, let us first attempt to be perfect parents.

About Child Discipline

Q - How should families take care of disciplining children?

First of all, we should be very clear that children are divine trusts to us and sprout from our own essence. For sensitive souls, the melodies of happiness at home begin with the soothing music of happy children.

As it is expressed in the traditions of the Prophet (peace and blessings be upon him), children are "flowers of Paradise," "fruit of hearts," and "divine blessings." Children are the best blessings of our Lord. How can anyone forget the joy at the birth of a first child? Children's smiles are like gifts from Paradise. For a mother to discipline, raise and contribute fine children to society is therefore the most honorable of occupations. A mother's heart is the first school of a child: here the child receives its basic training. In addition, righteous generations raised with great care will be protective shields between their parents and Hellfire. One of the most important duties of parents is to equip their children with Islamic virtues and good character. Yet it is not merely the central duty of parents to raise faithful and upright children: it also is a guarantee of receiving continuous rewards until the end of time.

Children are exceptional fruits of family happiness and a strong connection between the mother and the father. They are the most valuable trusts of Allah to the parents. People's responsibilities are expressed in the following saying of the Prophet (peace and blessings be upon him):

All of you are guardians and are responsible for your charges: … a man is a guardian of his family and is responsible for his charge; and a woman is guardian of the household of her husband and is responsible for her charge … (Bukhari, *Wasaya*, 9; Muslim, *Imara*, 20)

The Qur'an says:

O you who believe! Save yourselves and your families from a fire whose fuel is men and stones … (66:6)

The Messenger of Allah (peace and blessings be upon him) explains this verse, saying:

Keep them away from committing the things prohibited by Allah the Almighty and encourage them to perform good deeds. That is the way to save them from Hellfire. (Alusi, XXVIII, 156)

About Child Discipline

Q - From what basis should childrearing begin? Can using physical punishment be an acceptable method of discipline? What is the role of family in discipline and about what should families be careful?

Discipline of children should begin with the training of parents; such an important job can only be successfully performed with the benefit of proper training. How can inadequate parents discipline their children? As the poet says,

He, himself, is a dodderer in need of help
How is he supposed to help others?

Thus if child discipline begins starts parent discipline, it will yield more effective results. Again, as it is expressed by the poet Seyri:

Father, pillar of the family, must be upright and strong
Mother, heart of the family, must be a rose, sweet and warm

With all this in mind, we can summarize the basic principles to which parents need to pay attention as follows:

a. A spiritually meaningful name must be given to the child. At the head of the rights of a child upon its parents comes "to be given a good name," because the meaning of the name influences the personality of the child. In other words, the meaning of the child's name manifests itself upon the child. In a narration reported by Tabari, it is stated:

"The Messenger of Allah (peace and blessings be upon him) had a milk camel brought and asked, "Who shall milk this camel?" A man stood up. The Messenger of Allah asked, "What is your name?" The man said "Murra (bitterness)."

The Messenger of Allah said to him, "Sit down."

Again he said, "Who shall milk it?" A man stood up and the Messenger of Allah asked, "What is your name?" He said, "Jamra (fire)."

The Messenger of Allah said, "Sit down."

Yet again he said, "Who milks this camel?" A man stood up and the Messenger of Allah asked him, "What is your name?" The man said, "Ya`ish (he lives)." Then the Messenger of Allah gave him the job of milking the camel.* (Tabarani, *Mu`jam, XXII, 277; Muwatta, *Isti'zan*, 24)

b. For the spiritual development of their children, parents must be very sensitive about the religious lawfulness of what they eat.

c. Children grow up by imitating their parents in every aspect of their lives. Imitation, learning from example, is the essential characteristic of children. This is why parents must display exemplary behavior for them to imitate. For instance, if a child grows up in a family environment where the parents always dispute, then he or she will be affected by the atmo-

About Child Discipline

sphere and will most likely become ill-tempered. A child raised up in a peaceful and tranquil environment, on the other hand, will most likely grow up with good manners and become a decent person.

d. Children's behavior must always be under their parents' control, yet children should never feel that they are being controlled. They should be prevented from doing, in secret, bad things that they cannot do openly. Otherwise their character weakens and they become two-faced. The first manifestation of this condition is lying and hypocrisy.

e. Children's good deeds should be praised and rewarded, but their mistakes also should not be ignored. Just as rewarding good behaviors tends to make those behaviors permanent, so leaving offenses unpunished similarly incorporates them into a child's character. Childhood errors need to be taken seriously, because repeated bad actions may turn into addictions.

f. Unnecessary and constant punishment also has a negative impact upon children. For instance, if a child accidentally breaks a utensil in the kitchen, he or she should not be reprimanded, because accidents happen to everybody. Punishing children for accidents will create resentment, which may lead them to resist right behaviors that parents approve: they will do the opposite of whatever they are told to do. Therefore parents must be very sensitive and must not punish their children for accidental mistakes. However, we should never ignore or tolerate mistakes that might affect their morality.

It is also very important, when correcting mistakes, to make it clear to the child what was wrong about the action. It is only when a child grasps and accepts a mistake that he or she will be ready to profit from education. Otherwise, the child will continue to think the action right and will begin to blame the parents for injustice.

g. Therefore, also, when religious obligations and prohibitions are taught, children must be convinced about their reasons.

h. Proper manners and moral principles are essential. Wealthy families in particular should be careful to teach their children to treat their friends nicely. Rudeness and arrogance should be prevented. It is helpful to teach them the story of Qarun from the 28th chapter of the Qur'an – in simple words, so that they can understand.

i. Within the limits of lawfulness, children should be allowed to "live their childhood." However, just as they should not be placed under too much pressure, they should also not be left too much to their own devices. Too much idleness leads the growing personality astray. Too much pressure, on the other hand, crushes character and makes children either timid or rebellious. Children at the age of puberty are particularly inclined to be rebellious against their parents. This is why parents need to make every effort to

About Child Discipline

fill their children's time with appropriate activities in order to raise them as virtuous people.

j. Children need to be reminded of the blessings of Allah the Almighty and should be accustomed to show gratitude. They need to be raised according to the principles illustrated by the life of the Prophet (peace and blessings be upon him).

k. From an early age, children should be encouraged to develop habits of "worshiping Allah and serving humanity." Beyond simple habit formation, they should also be taught the *meaning* of our obligations of worship and service.

In short, if we want perfect children, let us first attempt to be perfect parents.

The true root of proper child discipline can only be parental love. Our children are entrusted to us by Allah; to love them and care for them is a means for us to reach happiness in this world and in the Hereafter. If we do not raise a decent generation, we will find ourselves alone in this world and later in the grave. We should not forget that the grave will be our ultimate residence. Let us treat our children accordingly!

Q - What should mothers be sensitive to with regard to a child's discipline and education?

As the proverb says, "A mother is a school." The mother's heart is the child's classroom. Because a mother stays with her children at home more often than anybody else, she will be the first and most effective role model to leave permanent traces in the souls of her children.

Every word coming out of a mother's mouth is like a brick in the edifice of the personality of her child. Mothers are the greatest source of mercy, the teachers of mercy. It becomes harder to educate children who are devoid of a mother's discipline, since discipline imposed without an underlying perception of mercy naturally produces rebellion. People of high character are usually to be found among those who were raised by a righteous mother.

A righteous and self-sacrificing mother, who shoulders many precious and difficult duties like the care of a home, the discipline of children and the thoughtful service of a husband, deserves immense love, deep respect and lifelong gratitude. Virtuous and serious Muslims from all over the Muslim lands have left us many beautiful illustrative examples of proper respect for mothers. First among these is, of course, the Messenger of Allah (peace and blessings be upon him). He visited his foster mother Halima (may Allah be pleased with her) every week. He used to lay his cloak on the ground and invite her to sit on it. Every time his foster mother entered the room, he stood up out of respect.

Mothers, who have the opportunity and time to be in close connection with their children, should

About Child Discipline

take hints about discipline and education from the lives of the Companions of the Prophet. Women Companions who were mothers got their own spiritual education from the Prophet. They used to counsel their children, too, to visit him regularly. Hudhayfa (may Allah be pleased with him) told this story:

One day mother one day asked me, "When was the last time that you visited the Prophet (peace and blessings be upon him)?"

I said, "I haven't seen him for a few days." She got very upset and reproached me. Finally I told her, "Please stop being angry at me! Let me go visit the Messenger of Allah (peace and blessings be upon him) right away and pray the evening prayer with him. Then I'll ask him to pray to Allah the Almighty for our forgiveness." (Tirmidhi, *Manaqib*, 30; Ahmad b. Hanbal, *Musnad*, V, 391-92)

We need to protect our children from extravagance and all kinds of extremism. We should give them respectable, meaningful names, introduce them to the Noble Qur'an and familiarize their pure hearts with the pleasures of praying, helping others and giving charity. We should also, as much as we can, avoid showing any kind of negative behavior that could increase selfishness in them. Children are like tape recorders. They are inclined to record and imitate everything they see. For instance, let's imagine what kind of damage the following incident could do, once recorded in a child's pure memory.

A Peaceful Home

A beggar, old and sick, knocks on the door of a family's home to ask for help. The father of the household reprimands the man; his daughter observes this. The little girl asks, "Daddy, why are you breaking the poor man's heart?"

The coldhearted father replies, "Don't pay attention to him! These kinds of people are not ashamed to be a burden on others. When they succeed in getting money, they just waste it. Maybe they are even richer than we are!"

Meanwhile, because of his dire need, the poor man at the door keeps asking, "For the sake of Allah, please help me!"

The father's anger grows worse. He shouts, "Get out of here, you shameless man!"

Perhaps some of us are acquainted with such scenes. But wouldn't any little girl who saw such a thing and loved her father, begin to lose her feelings of compassion? Is it not likely that she herself might become a coldhearted person who feels nothing for the sufferings of the others?

Mindful of the educational effects of actions, when my own father Musa Efendi (may Allah bless his soul) wanted to give something to a needy person, he sometimes gave it through the hands of children. In this way we all became accustomed to helping others. On one occasion, people came around collecting donations for an important cause. My father watched

About Child Discipline

the seven-year-old boy sitting next to him. The little boy, unaware of being observed, dropped his small amount of pocket money into the donation box. He had obviously been affected by the generosity of the adults around him. After my father saw what the little boy did, he called him aside. After praising his good deed, he told the child, "You did well, my boy! If you hadn't given anything, it would have made me sad."

This story is just one example of the many we might call to mind, all of which prove how children imitate the acts of the adults around them.

We should keep in mind that traditions of the Prophet suggest that girls need more attention than boys. The Prophet (peace and blessings be upon him) says:

Anyone who has three daughters and provides for them, clothes them, shows mercy to them, assists in their marriages and keeps assisting them afterwards, will definitely enter Paradise. (Abu Dawud, *Adab*, 121; Ibn Hanbal, III, 97)

and

"If someone raises two girls to maturity in kindness, on the Day of Resurrection, he and I will be like this" – and he interlaced his fingers (to show the degree of nearness between him and that person). (Muslim, *Birr*, 149; See also Tirmidhi, *Birr*, 13)

This narration informs us how we should treat our children, especially our daughters.

Another important point with regard to child-rearing is the matter of physical abuse. The beating of children cannot be accepted under any circumstances. In order to prevent children's bad behavior, some precautions may be taken, but beating can never be among them. Beating turns our young people – our future! – either into cowards, or into indecent and shameless people. It is clear that the Prophet (peace and blessings be upon him) prohibited beating even in the discipline of animals, let alone human beings. When our mother `A'isha was given a camel as a gift, he warned her about training it in these words:

"O `A'isha! Kindness is not found in anything without adding to its beauty and is not withdrawn from anything without making it defective." (Muslim, *Birr*, 78; See also Abu Dawud, *Adab*, 10)

A mother's heart can control the outbursts of family members, especially the obstinacy of her children.

A pious mother is like an embrace of divine mercy. That is why the Prophet said: *"Paradise is under the feet of mothers..."* Since the seeds of our happiness are sown in the hearts of our mothers, the Messenger of Allah insisted upon love for mothers. When he (peace and blessings be upon him) was asked who is most entitled to be treated with the highest respect, he said three times, "Your mother." Only after that did he say, "Your father." (Bukhari, *Adab*, 2; Muslim, *Birr*,

1, 2; See also Ibn Maja, *Wasaya*, 4; Abu Dawud, *Adab*, 120; Tirmidhi, *Birr*, 1)

> *Q - How should a woman treat her husband's children from his earlier marriage(s)?*

She should accept them as if they were her own children. It is important that she not hold her attention, compassion, mercy and service away from them. All his life, the Prophet showed respect to the mother of Hadrat `Ali, Fatima bint Asad (may Allah be pleased with them both), because she had protected him and treated him (peace and blessings be upon him), like her own son. When she passed away, the Prophet prayed over her body, saying:

O my mother! May Allah have mercy on your soul. You were my second mother after my real mother. You would stay hungry, yet feed me; you would not clothe yourself, yet you clothed me; you would hold yourself away from good food, yet you let me eat it; and in doing all this, you sought nothing other than Allah's contentment and eternal salvation.

The Prophet ordered the body to be washed three times. Then he dressed her with his own shirt; she was enshrouded wearing his shirt. The Messenger of Allah helped in digging her grave and afterwards he lay down in it and prayed for her. (Tabarani, *Mu'jam al-Kabir*, XXIV, 351-52; Hakim, III, 116-17)

The Prophet's love, respect and gratitude for his foster mother's care should certainly be an example for us. Yet, let us not forget how fine an example is set by his foster mother's compassion, care, education, gentle treatment and kind words toward him! By taking pains and leaving precious memories in the mind of an orphan, this great mother won the veneration of a people, as well as eternal divine mercy.

Let us not neglect to mention that fathers, too, should be mature enough to treat their wives' children by previous marriages in the same fashion as their own children if they are to live together.

> *Q - Could you give us some examples from the life of our Prophet (peace and blessings be upon him) illustrating his dealing with children?*

The Messenger of Allah (peace and blessings be upon him) always treated children with compassion. He used to kiss them and comb their hairs with his fingers. He was not fond of people who did not show affection to children; he considered them rude and harsh.

According to the report of `A'isha (may Allah be pleased with her), one day the Prophet was playing with his grandsons and kissing them. A Bedouin came up to him and remarked,

About Child Discipline

"You (people) kiss the children! We don't kiss them."

The Prophet said, *"I cannot put mercy in your heart after Allah has taken it away from it."* (Bukhari, *Adab*, 22)

On a similar occasion, Allah's Apostle kissed his grandson al-Hasan bin `Ali while al-Aqra' bin Habis at-Tamim was sitting beside him. Al-Aqra' said, "I have ten children and I have never kissed a single one of them."

Allah's Messenger cast a look at him and said, *"Whoever is not merciful to others will not be treated mercifully."*

If we take a lesson from these traditions, we see that Muslims' hearts should be full of affection, love and mercy toward children, who are Allah's trusts to us. We should also be aware of where and how we are supposed to manifest our love and mercy.

Once, the Prophet was holding his small grandson in his lap when the child urinated on him. Umm Fadl (may Allah be pleased with her) was shocked and began to scold the boy. The Prophet (peace and blessings be upon him) stopped her, saying, *"You're hurting my son! May Allah have mercy on you."* In this way he gave a strong example of the importance of tolerating the inadvertent offenses of children.

Sometimes the Messenger of Allah prayed while his grandsons were on his lap and sometimes he let them climb on his back while he was prostrating. He told the Companions who wanted to interfere, *"Let the boys have fun."*

Again, once when the Messenger of Allah heard a child crying during formal prayers, he shortened the prayer as much as possible. Afterwards he told the congregation, *"Don't you know that their crying makes me sad?"*

Anas (may Allah be pleased with him), who served the Prophet as a young boy, narrates:

I served the Messenger of Allah (peace and blessings be upon him) for ten years and, by Allah, he never said to me a single harsh word and he never asked me about anything why I had done that, or why I had not done that. (Bukhari, Sawm, 53; Manaqib, 23; Muslim, Fada`il, 82)

Children who were raised next to the Prophet were adorned with special beauties and insights. Another exemplary incident is the report narrated by Sahl b. Sa`d (may Allah be pleased with him):

Allah's Messenger was offered something to drink and drank some of it. On his right was a boy and on his left were some elderly people. He said to the boy, *"May I give this to these older people first?"*

The young boy was very wise and said, *"O Messenger of Allah! I will not give up my share from you to somebody else."* Upon hearing that, the Messenger of Allah (peace and blessings be upon him) placed

About Child Discipline

the cup in the hand of that boy at the expense of the elderly Companions. (Bukhari, *Ashriba'*, 19)

In another report:

On a day when the Prophet was staying at the house of his daughter Fatima, his grandsons, Hasan and Husayn, asked him for some water (may Allah be pleased with them all). Allah's Messenger gave the water first to Hasan. From this, Fatima guessed that the Prophet loved Hasan more. The Messenger of Allah said, *"No, Hasan was the first to ask for water."* And then he added: *"When it comes to gifts, treat your children equally. If I had wanted to privilege anyone over others, I would have preferred girls."* (Ibn Hanbal, I, 101; Ibn Hajar, *al-Matalib al-'Aliya*, IV, 69; Haythami, IV, 153)

Our Prophet emphasized the significance of child discipline in many of his sayings.

Give treats to your children and raise them well. (Ibn Maja, *Adab*, 3)

A father cannot give his child a better gift than good discipline. (Tirmidhi, *Birr*, 33)

It is better for a Muslim to instruct his [or her] child in even one good characteristic than to give a heaping measure of food in charity. (Tirmidhi, *Birr*, 33)

When a person dies, all of his acts come to an end but three: charity that recurs, knowledge that brings benefit, or a pious child who prays for him. (Muslim, *Wasiyya*, 14; Tirmidhi, *Ahkam*, 36)

— A Peaceful Home

Among the rights of a child upon his [or her] father are a spiritually meaningful name and good manners (Bayhaqi, *Shu`ab al-Iman*, VI, 401-02)

Anyone who has three daughters and provides for them, clothes them, shows mercy to them, assists in their marriages and keeps assisting them afterwards, will definitely enter Paradise. (Abu Dawud, *Adab,* 121; Ibn Hanbal, III, 97)

"If someone raises two girls to maturity in kindness, on the Day of Resurrection, he and I will be like this" – and he interlaced his fingers (to show the degree of nearness between him and that person). (Muslim, *Birr,* 149; See also Tirmidhi, *Birr,* 13)

If someone has three daughters and is patient with them and clothes them from his wealth, they will be a shield against the Fire for him. (Bukhari, *Zakat,* 10; *Adab,* 18; Muslim, *Birr,* 147; See also Tirmidhi, *Birr,* 13)

> *Q - Are there any other Companions who, like Anas, were raised by the Prophet?*

There are many Companions like Anas. 'Ali (may Allah be pleased with him) comes at the head of the list. 'Ali was one of the Prophet's first cousins. He filled his soul with wisdom under the auspices of the Messenger of Allah. `Ali became the gate of knowledge and the first link in the chain of Sufi masters, a lineage that will continue until the end of days.

About Child Discipline

`Ali's brother Ja`far al-Tayyar was another exemplary manifestation of love for the Prophet and was also spiritually reared by him.

Fatima, the daughter of the Messenger of Allah, became the great lady of the Muslims. Because of her high manners and her compassionate protection of her blessed father, she was called "the mother of her father." One of her sons, Hasan, became the crown of the lineage of Sayyids and the other, Husayn, became the crown of the lineage of Sharifs.

Mus`ab b. Umayr (may Allah be pleased with him) refused the wealth of his pagan family and preferred to be next to the Prophet. He became a matchless symbol of altruism and sacrifice. His love for Allah's Messenger was so great that he even gave his life for him.

Usama b. Zayd was appointed as the commander of the Muslim army when he was twenty years old.

There are many more young Companions who were trained by the Prophet (peace and blessings be upon him), but I think these examples are enough for now.

Q - Sir, if you don't mind, we also would like to hear to some reminiscences from your own childhood years.

Everybody naturally retains many stories from

A Peaceful Home

childhood. Some of them leave deep marks. I would like to share some of my memories.

My childhood passed in Erenkoy. In those days there were gardens around the houses. On the first floors of the houses there were rooms for the entertainment of guests and these were the sites of many friendly and lively gatherings.

Houses were especially filled with guests for fast-break dinners during the month of Ramadan. Every night people from different walks of life used to be invited for these *iftar* dinners. After dinner, the guests were presented with gifts that were commonly known as "tooth rent." Depending on the guests, the gift sometimes was a length of fabric and sometimes was a sum of money in an envelope. After the special Ramadan *tarawih* prayer, hot tea was served and all the guests chatted about their own worlds. Those were wonderful times of socializing and joining of hearts.

Another wonderful thing in those days was the relations of the neighbors. People treated their neighbors like relatives. We (I mean the children) used to confuse who was a relative and who was a neighbor. Wealthy neighbors embraced the needy ones with compassion. Residents of the neighborhood acted together to take care of the needs of the poor and to help the girls make their wedding preparations.

In those days, tuberculosis was a common epidemic. There was not enough medicine. Residents of

About Child Discipline

the neighborhood felt sorry for the sick people. Patients were treated in hospitals located in the woods, because it was the only place they could breathe fresh air and feel better. Unfortunately, dying at an early age was a common. Compassionate neighbors gave the patients food, which was believed to strengthen their blood.

Visiting the sick was the first thing for any family to do. Depending on their financial means, they took soup or dessert with them and their visits were short.

Funerals were similar. Prayers used to be said in congregation. For three days, food was prepared for the household of the deceased by the neighbors.

Fifty years ago, a refrigerator was a very rare appliance. In order to keep something cool, it used be placed in a jar and lowered down in a well. Neighbors who own a refrigerator used to give their neighbors ice in the evening. It was the duty of the children to take the ice to the neighbors. In this way they were accustomed to altruism, charity, solidarity and serving others at a very early age.

In my childhood, the coast of Erenkoy was not so crowded. There was a two-meter-wide beach on the coast. We used to make sandcastles on the beach. Sometimes we had fights about the boundaries of our castles. We would blame each other, saying, "You trespassed across my borders – no, you crossed into mine!" Eventually a wave would come and destroy

A Peaceful Home

all of our castles. When I look back, I see that there is little difference between our childhood fights and the fights of older people. When people get old, they become slaves to selfish pleasures; however, in the end, everything goes with the wave of the last breath.

The most exiting day was the day when the *adhan* or call to prayer was returned from Turkish to its original Arabic form. Everybody woke up early at dawn to listen to the call for the dawn prayer. That night was like the night of a holiday.[5] It was like the day when Bilal Habashi (may Allah be pleased with him) went to recite the very first *adhan*. It was as if the morning breeze were carrying the tune of the *adhan* from Medina. To hear the *adhan* in its Arabic form had been an ardent longing in the hearts of our people. Hearing it brought the sort of feeling that people feel when they are coming back from a journey abroad. May Allah protect our *adhan* and our flag, our country and our nation, from all kinds of dangers. May He keep us far away from all types of evil. *Amin!*

Q - Were there any personalities who affected you in your childhood?

The two great figures who affected me most in childhood were my mom and dad. In addition, I also had a very pleasant environment.

---

5. In 1930s and 1940s, *adhan* used to be recited in Tur-ish, but after eighteen years it was returned to its original Arabic form on June 16th 1950 by Prime Minister Adnan Menderes.

About Child Discipline

My mother was like an angel. At every opportunity, she would inspire us with love for the friends of Allah. She adorned our hearts with spiritual beauties. After she had her second child, she memorized the whole Qur'an. Her admiration and love for the Noble Qur'an have always influenced me deeply.

My father, on the other hand, (may Allah bless his soul) was a monumental personality in my life. With his exemplary love for Allah, sincerity, piety, manners and dignity, he was a man of lofty horizons. In those days the Imam Hatip High Schools[6] had only recently been founded and there were not many opportunities for their graduates. Nonetheless our father, with great joy, registered us to an Imam Hatip High School. We stayed in the school dormitory in our senior year. Our teachers took us on school trips to historical sites, mosques and Ottoman palaces. This taught us about what our predecessors had done for the sake of Islam and the country. They always urged us to be a generation worthy to be their successors. From time to time they took us to visit contemporary religious scholars and so introduced us to men of high spirituality.

My father's love for the poor was like a vast sea. When poor people accepted his help, he would go to visit them in a mood of thankfulness. When he gave them money, he would place it in an envelope on which he wrote, "Thank you for accepting this."

---

6. This is a type of Turkish religious school.

This attitude of spiritual grace and elegance was the result of helping creatures for the sake of their Creator. Together with my mom, my father used to prepare food and take it to the hospitals. I was not aware at the time, but these manifestations of mercy made a beautiful impression on my soul. In short, my parents were a source of mercy and blessing for me.

Many of my other memories are from my years at Imam Hatip High School. We were very lucky in our teachers. We had the chance to get to know many unforgettable figures. Here are some of them.

Celâleddin Öktem was a 70-year-old teacher who had Parkinson's syndrome. Despite his old age and his illness, he came to class regularly and taught like a 25-year -old.

Abdülkadir Keçeoğlu, who was also known as Yaman Dede, was a convert from the Eastern Orthodox Church. He used to start class by teaching ten or fifteen minutes of Persian grammar; then he would begin to recite verses from Rumi's *Mathnawi*. For the rest of the class he would interpret the verses while shedding tears of spiritual ecstasy. Deep depressions had formed under his eyes because of his tears. His soul was filled with love for the Messenger of Allah (peace and blessings be upon him). When he was asked about how much he loved Rumi, he used to respond, "How could I not love Rumi, my son! He took my hand and led me to the Prophet!" Many years have passed since then, but the traces he left in

About Child Discipline

our souls are still fresh. His tears when reciting the lines, *"Cheer us with your beauty, I am burning, O Messenger of Allah!"* from Rumi's famous poem, are still in front of my eyes.

Another teacher used to come to school at seven in the morning and prepare our meals. Still another would warn us not to waste our food, but to think about the unfortunate people around the world. He would give us this advice in a very kind and gentle manner.

Our philosophy teacher, *Nurettin Topçu*, was really worried about the egoism and selfishness of people in modern society. He saw the Sufi path as a cure for these problems. He used to exclaim in astonishment, "How can these people stay away from Sufism?"

One teacher gave calligraphy classes and supplied the ink and reed pens for the poor students out of his own pocket.

Another used to walk through the dormitory at night and put blankets over the students to keep them warm.

Still other teachers gave supplementary classes after school, so as to help students get a better education.

The most significant thing that all our teachers were trying to teach us was to know how to employ our lives and property rightly, in the way of Islam. They demonstrated this in their own actions.

Since then forty years have passed; however, the good examples they left for us are still intact. For that, I always pray for them. May Allah be pleased with them all! Now it is our turn. It is time to beautify today and tomorrow. This is our duty and may Allah grant us success in our duty.

> *Q – Sir, talking about today, could you tell us what kinds of dangers lie in wait for our children? What is the responsibility of parents in the face of these dangers?*

One-sided education comes at the head of the dangers awaiting our youth. If material education is not supported by spiritual discipline, both of the child's worlds will be ruined. We need to be aware that a generation that has not been formed for spiritual qualities and beauties cannot attain happiness, even if it gathers to itself every kind of diploma in the world. We can observe many pitiable results of such one-sided education.

Then there are the many perilous addictions in the contemporary world. Those who ruin their lives because of drugs and those who do not protect their honor but fall into the pits of prostitution, are among the unfortunate examples. They show us what kinds

About Child Discipline

of dangers await our children. If we can feel those dangers, we can also see that their cure lies in placing faith and good morals in the hearts of the young. How can hearts which do not carry the light of revelation find real happiness? In this regard, we should contemplate the meaning of these lines of Turkish poet Mehmet Akif Ersoy:

> *O Lord! Faith is the greatest essence in the heart*
> *A heart without faith is a burden in the chest.*

Ignorance in religious matters is a horrible darkness. People are enemies of what they do not know. Moving away from religion causes spiritual deterioration and narrows the horizons of the heart. It kills the power of insight. It deprives us of the subtleties and spiritual guidance of the Holy Qur'an and the Sunna. It causes us to lose track our divine essence and turns the person into a bag of skin filled with meat and bones. And as a result, the human being becomes a selfish creature.

There is a well-known story told among the common people in Turkey. A father notices that his son is weak in religion and virtue. He warns him, "You cannot become a man!" However, the boy carries on in the direction he was heading, goes to school and to university and eventually becomes governor of the province. Then he sends his guards to bring his father to his palatial office.

When his father appears, he boasts, "Look, Dad! You once told me that I could not even become a man, but I have become Governor!"

His father sadly responds, "My dear son, I didn't say that you couldn't become a governor. I said that you couldn't become a man. And if you were truly a man, you would never drag your father here. You would go to him."

The situation of so many of us is the same as the situation of the son in this story. Neglecting spiritual discipline leads us to abandon religion and virtue in order to idolize material success. But Idolizing material success is not wisdom; it is stupidity. It is not healing, but disease and oppression. It means numbing our spirituality and turning the community into a corpse. It means to bury people under rocks and soil even before they are dead.

In order to reach the honor and dignity of being human, we must heed the warnings of the Noble Qur'an. Allah the Almighty states His greatest blessing to mankind as follows:

Allah the All-Merciful taught the Qur'an. He created the human being and taught him clarity... and the heaven, He raised it high and He set up the Balance. (55:1-4, 7)

Our Lord, who created a balance in the universe, informs us that there is trial and weighing not only in this world but also in the next. Here and Hereafter

About Child Discipline

alike have scales that measure one's quality. Life and death are two different but inseparable and accurate measures. If we are to truly succeed, all of our states must fall within the limits of these measures and be an example for following generations. In another verse, it is expressed that:

So whoever has done an atom's weight of good shall see it. And whoever has done an atom's weight of evil shall see it. (99: 7-8)

How heedless are those who continue to live haphazardly, without self-evaluation, while the universe is constructed in perfect measure!

In light of the aforementioned verse from Sura 55 of the Qur'an, we should explain to our children the wisdom of creation, the text of the Noble Qur'an and the meaning of service to Allah the Almighty. In short, we must educate our youth to protect their perfect and dignified position as human beings and not to upset the divine balance. With the help of Allah, a good family with skilled parents can achieve this.

Parents who think seriously about the future of their children will certainly undertake this task. Of course, I am not talking about their future in this world alone, but also their eternal future. Unfortunately, today, in order to increase youths' worldly prospects, we often put their eternal future in danger. Parents tolerate many wrong actions by saying, "What can we do? Our kids' future is more important!" This sort of attitude leads young people into committing sins and rebellion against Allah. Meanwhile, the more we raise our children according to the principles of Islam, the better the future prepared for them by Allah the Almighty will be. That is the secret behind the expansion of the Ottoman state over more than 24 million square meters of land. That is how divine help reached those people at many different times. Some of the last manifestations of this reality occurred in the War of Turkish Independence and the Battle of the Dardanelles. How nicely Mehmet Akif expresses this:

Extracting the rules directly from the Qur'an
We need to make the era speak about Islam.

Therefore we have to raise our children with morals, ideals and the straight path of the Qur'an. Then they will be individuals who are beneficial to themselves, their country, their community and most importantly to their religion. Again, Mehmet Akif explains this in the following lines:

The demise of an abandoned land is justified.
It will not be spiritually desolated if you do something about it.

As we mentioned before, the spiritual education that underlies national greatness is the responsibility of parents. It should be remembered that although many great victories, such as the War of Independence and the Battle of the Dardanelles, look like the undertakings of brave soldiers, commanders and

About Child Discipline

martyrs. In fact they are the work of the parents who raised and sent those soldiers to the battlefield.

> *Q - While some families try everything to have a child, others do not want children and try everything not to have any. Is this an appropriate action?*

Those who marry but do not want to have children without a valid and absolutely necessary reason and try to kill them in the womb with certain interference, are in fact killing the next generation. Plants and animals display many incredible and persistent ways to procreate. How can we reasonably explain the attempts of human beings, who are the best of the creation, to annihilate their own future? Even a snake hides its eggs in a safe place and protects them. What a pity when the greatest of creatures lacks a snake's feeling of mercy and compassion!

The Qur'an depicts the scene of the Judgment Day is depicted as follows:

And when the female infant buried alive is asked for what sin she was killed... (81:8-9)

That sort of murder, which took place routinely about fourteen hundred years ago, has changed its shape in the contemporary world and started to repeat in the disgraceful form of abortion. Today some parents, without any valid reason beyond their own selfish convenience and comfort, attempt to abort their children. It is as if they are in a murder competition with the wild people of the age of the ignorance before Islam, who used to bury their daughters alive. Unborn children are torn into pieces in the mother's womb for the sake of nothing. Before anything else, this is a form of ingratitude for a divine blessing. Who can tell? Perhaps those who commit this crime will remain all alone in this world; the children they do have may not lift a hand to help them. They should also think about what would have happened if their own parents had entertained the same ideas about them. They would never have been born.

The pages of history repeatedly show us the sad ends of those who lived their lives merely as physical bodies – those who had no faith and religious feelings, those who had no ideals but to satisfy their mundane desires and those who abandoned all human honor and dignity.

May Allah bless us and help us to found our families upon goodness. May He bestow upon us wonderful progeny who will serve both the Muslims and all humanity.

Amin!

The Place of Women in Islam and the Education of females

Women's dignity and chastity turns society into a Paradise. Generations raised in that Paradise become society's source of peace. Thus a righteous woman is like a crystal chandelier, shedding light in the family.

The Place of Women in Islam

Q - What is the place of women in Islam? In the contemporary world, deceptive fancy words push women into the streets to look for happiness. But where should women look for happiness?

Allah the Almighty created women as emotionally deeper and stronger than men. This emotional depth is the natural requirement of women's primary task, the protection and education of human progeny. When the value of this divine appointment is ignored, a woman's nature is betrayed.

Today, a false competition has arisen between men and women. But competition is contrary to the design of human beings, who are made to cooperate with each other. When women's service as wives and mothers is not respected, then peace and tranquility at home are lost; social life is shaken; and individuals lose their personalities.

Because women's and men's physical and spiritual features are not identical, they cannot usefully be claimed to be practically and legally equal. The important matter is not a literal equality between the sexes, but a balanced distribution of rights and responsibilities.

Allah the Almighty created an equitable distribution of tasks between men and women. He appointed them different but complementary family roles. When men and women are materially and spiritually united with each other, a maturity appropriate to their respective roles arises and then family and society alike reach peace and tranquility.

The maturity of a woman appears when she protects and develops the beautiful features that Allah has bestowed upon her so as to bring depth and refinement into her family. If she loses sight of this possibility, abandoning her own real experience for what others tell her is her nature, she loses her dignity and devastates her social value. Slowly grace, gentleness and sincerity become impossible for everyone and ultimately society becomes more like a desert.

But when women are able to live according to their own authentic experience and natures, they can turn society into Paradise. Woman is like a crystal chandelier, shedding light over society. If we turn the pages of history, we can see that societies rise and fall with the status of their women. If only the streets appear to women as sources of happiness, then the paths of life will be strewn with shards of glass.

The Place of Women in Islam

Women's happiness lies hidden in the reverence shown them by their families. The famous saying of the Prophet (peace and blessings be upon him), is crucial:

Paradise lies under the feet of mothers.[7] (Suyuti, *Jami' al-Saghir*, I, 125)

This unconditional call for respect is the greatest news for mothers everywhere.

A virtuous mother is the divine embrace of mercy, the source of her family's joy, the light of pleasure and delight and the focus of every family member's compassion. She is the exceptional and carefully selected manifestation of Our Lord's key names "the All-Merciful" and "the Most Compassionate."

There is no other being created who deserves our admiration and love as much as our mothers do. They carry us for nine months in their bellies, for a few years in their arms and for a lifetime in their hearts. And mothers who shoulder housework and childrearing really deserve endless love, deep respect and lifelong gratitude.

---

7. A similar hadith runs as follows:
   A Companion named Jahima came to the Prophet and said:
   "O Messenger of Allah! I would like to go to war with the Muslim army. I came here to talk to you about it."
   Allah's Messenger asked him, "Is your mother alive?"
   He said: "Yes, she is."
   Then the Messenger of Allah said, "Then serve your mother, because Paradise is under her feet." (Nasa'i, *Jihad*, 6)

Is there any device to measure the level of endless sacrifice in our mother's heart? She didn't eat so that we might eat; she didn't clothe herself so that we might be clothed; she didn't sleep, so that we might sleep well at night. Is it possible to pay our debts to our mothers (and fathers) who would do everything they could not to see us hurt?

Rumi says, "Be careful about your mother's right: make her the crown of your head. If there were no mothers' labor pains, babies would find no way into the world."

Abu Hanifa, a great friend of Allah and a legal scholar, refused to be the judge of Baghdad in order not to participate in the oppression of the government. Caliph Abu Ja`far al-Mansur put him in jail and had him whipped. Every day he had the numbers of lashes increased. Abu Hanifa was worried not for the pain of the lashes, but for what his mother might feel if she learned he was in prison. He sent a message to his friends: "Please do not let my mother hear of my situation. She could not endure it if she knew of my suffering. She would be devastated and I cannot bear to see her sad." Abu Hanifa expressed here a prime example of a mother's compassion. Note too that his love for his mother lessened his concern for his own pain.

Another example is displayed in Bahauddin Naqshband's saying, "Let those who wish to visit our grave visit our mother's grave first."

The Place of Women in Islam

It was Abdurrahman Molla Jami`, another Naqshi master, who first said, "How can I not love my mother? She carried me for nine months in her belly, then for awhile in her arms and finally for a lifetime in her heart."

Q - What is the importance of mothers in raising the younger generation?

Guessing a nation's future is not miraculous. It is enough to look at the state of its youth. Youth in every era of history have looked for excitement, for a way to spend their energy. This quest is like society's heartbeat. In other words, every nation takes shape according to the ideals and feelings of its youth. If a nation's youth spend their time and energy on good deeds, then that nation's future becomes secure. On the contrary, if a nation's youth spend their time and energy on selfish deeds and become the slaves of their desires, then that nation moves toward disappointment and loss. Therefore mothers in particular must be very careful in parenting the future generation. All of the friends of Allah and the great statesmen of history, got their first discipline from pious mothers.

The best examples for how this works come from the female Companions. They taught their children altruism and sacrifice in every way they could. They also filled the souls of their children with love for Allah and His Messenger. Thus they proved that strong nations are created from strong families. And strong families, in turn, are the works of righteous women, who pass through a spiritual education and eliminate their petty desires.

> *Q - What is the role of Qur'anic schools in girls' education? And what are the most important issues requiring educational attention in these schools?*

All institutions, especially those responsible for spiritual education, like Qur'anic schools, must be places of compassion, altruism and service. More than just giving information, schools should inspire students with love, mercy and the excitement of serving others. Insensitive teachers who cannot make the little hearts under their tutelage feel the joys of faith and love for the Qur'an, are under a heavy responsibility. The schools they teach at belong to the entire Muslim community and their students are merely entrusted to them. If they cannot give their charges a proper education, they will be liable for those students' rights in the Hereafter.

In the contemporary world, where many people are enslaved by materialism, Qur'an teachers must be more sensitive toward their students. They should seek first of all to fill the hearts of their students with love and respect for their teachers. Before even starting to teach the alphabet of the Qur'an, they should inspire their students with the grandeur and importance of the work of study. They should fill their students' young hearts with love for Allah and His Messenger. They should be able to manifest grace and refinement and the many varieties of beauty present in Islam, through their own pure hearts.

Qur'anic teachers who act sometimes like judges and sometimes like executioners and who attempt to establish their authority through force and stern faces, are wasting their efforts. Such an attitude is a great mistake. There is, in fact, not a greater mistake to be made than turning people away from Qur'anic education and consequently darkening their lives.

Teachers and their assistants should learn how to be of mature service to the people. A mature servant has a heart is full of wisdom. Mature servants are merciful, altruistic and upright, as well as being people of action. They are enemies of hatred. Also, mature servants should be able to protect their faith and personalities under any circumstances and therefore able to have a positive effect on whomever may be around them.

Mature servants are able to keep their hearts free from the love of property, the love of position and the obsession with profit. As the Sufi saying goes:

This world becomes a paradise through three practices:

- offering charity with hands, tongue and heart

- forgiving, rather than criticizing, the servants of Allah;

- not reciprocating the oppression of oppressors, but helping them to understand and correct their mistakes.

According to another Sufi saying, good people are to be found in the following three groups:

- Those who do not hurt anybody;

- Those who are too modest to hear their good qualities from others;

- Those who see the creation as a divine trust and who look at creatures through the eyes of their Creator.

Just as scenes of flowers and roses can make even the harshest person smile, so the souls of those who are hoping to guide society should spread happiness to the people around them. Even the hardest and the most despicable hearts should be moved to wake up and soften before them.

The primary aim of Qur'anic schools for girls should be the moral education of their students rather than their material education, because tomorrow's foremost mothers will be among the graduates of these schools. When girls graduate, they should be able to display the beauties of Islam.

Qur'anic school must be adorned with the spirits of two Fatimas.[8]

> *Q - Who are these two Fatimas? Could you elaborate, please?*

The first Fatima is the one whose virtues are mentioned in Sura 76, verses 8-11. When Hasan and Husayn (may Allah be pleased with them) were children, they got very sick. Their parents 'Ali and Fatima (may Allah be pleased with them) offered three days of fasting as a prayer for the children's health. On the first day, when they wanted to break their fast at dinnertime, a poor man came by and asked, "Please give me something to eat, for the sake of Allah!" They gave him all the food on the table. Then they broke their fast with water.

On the second day, an orphan came to their door and asked, "Please give me something to eat for the sake of Allah!" Again they gave him all the food on the table and broke their fast with water. Later, they began the next day's fasting with no more than water, too.

On the third day, around the same time, a slave came to their door and asked food. Again they gave

---

8. The author of this book, Osman Nuri Efendi, assisted in the opening of many Qur'anic schools for boys and girls. This is why he emphasizes the significance of good behavior in teachers of the Qur'an and the importance of their being compassionate and loving.

him all the food on the table and broke their fast with water. Then the following verses were revealed:

And they give food out of love for Him to the poor and the orphan and the captive:" Surely we fear from our Lord a stern, distressful day!" Therefore Allah will guard them from the evil of that day and cause them to meet with ease and happiness; and reward them, because they were patient, with garden and silk. [9]

There are three things in these verses that should attract our attention.

First, they call for us to be able to see the creation through the eyes of the Creator and to be able to make the needy happy. In this regard Abu Bakr al-Warraq (may Allah bless his soul) says:

Those who do not give in charity should not claim that they will attain Paradise. Those who do not love the poor should not claim that they love the Messenger of Allah (peace and blessings be upon him). Both of these claimants are liars.

Second, the verses advise us to give our charity for the pleasure of Allah the Almighty alone. 'Ali and Fatima (may Allah be pleased with them) used to say, "We do not expect anything in return. We do not expect gratitude. We give in charity just for the contentment of Allah the Almighty." We should do

---

9. This is the origin of 76:8-12, according to Wahidi, p. 470; Zamakhshari, VI, 191-92; and Razi, XXX, 244).

the same and expect nothing in return from the servants of Allah.

The third thing to notice is that these reverend and exemplary people say, *"We fear for the Day of Judgment."* This is the state of hearts that are filled with awe of Allah. Approving such sincerity and service, Allah the Almighty responds, *"We will protect them from the calamities of that Day."*

Another example that manifests the spiritual world of our first Fatima is her love and sacrifice for the Prophet.

Once the Prophet was offering his prayer in the shade of the Ka`ba. His great enemy Abu Jahl happened to come by; he was happy to catch the Prophet alone. Abu Jahl and some other members of the Quraysh tribe who were with him immediately sent somebody to fetch the abdominal contents of a recently slaughtered camel. When the filthy guts arrived, those wretched men dumped them over the Prophet (peace and blessings be upon him) while he was making his prostration. The Prophet's uncle `Abbas, who was not a Muslim at the time, saw what had just happened, but felt unable to speak up against his fellow tribesmen. Just then Fatima, who was only about nine or ten years old at the time, ran into the sanctuary and began struggling to pull the steaming offal away from her father, crying the whole time. The Messenger of Allah (peace and blessings be upon him) finished his prayer and comforted her, urging her not to cry." (See Bukhari, *Salat*, 109, *Jihad*, 98, *Jizya*, 21; Muslim, *Jihad*, 107)

Fatima was so brave that she could stand up against the idolaters. Even 'Abbas, the Prophet's uncle, dared not do that, even though the Arabs are known for making sacrifices for their relatives. Fatima loved Allah and His Messenger more than anything else. This is why she is often called *Umm Abiha:* "the mother of her father."

Our second exemplary Fatima is the one who stopped 'Umar (may Allah be pleased with him) when he was on his way to kill the Prophet. She became the reason for 'Umar's conversion to Islam. On that day, she recited the Qur'an so devoutly that a coldhearted person like 'Umar found himself softening, so that he began to weep out of compassion.

It is very important for the girls in these schools to take the two Fatimas as role models. Each and every girl should be generous and altruistic, should perform her deeds for Allah's sake and should recite the Qur'an with joy and spirit. When our girls resemble the two Fatimas, they will be able to achieve every desired objective.

Nor should we forget our mother `A'isha (may Allah be pleased with her). She was the most intelligent of the wives of the Prophet and was accepted as one of the seven legal scholars among the Companions. Allah's Messenger (peace and blessings be upon him) said about her:

"Learn one third of your religion from `A'isha."
(Daylami, II, 165/2828)

Therefore every Muslim woman should aim to take lessons from the intuition, chastity and intelligence of our mother `A'isha.

Our supplication from our Lord is to be blessed with daughters who have the heart of our mother Fatima, the intelligence and chastity of our mother `A'isha and especially the altruism and fidelity of our mother Khadija (may Allah be pleased with them all).

Amin!

Some Ottoman Examples

The Ottomans took their place in history not just through being a magnificent state, but also through being a civilization of endowments.

Some Ottoman Examples

> *Q - Sir, could you give us some examples from later periods of Islamic history? Did Muslims in later ages live Islam as the Companions did?*

Islam is a dynamic religion. This is why the beauties that existed in its earliest days have continued to live up until today, even though there have been some changes.

The age of the Ottomans, in particular, was like a second *`asr al-sa`ada*[10]. Our predecessors used to compete with each other in the performance of good deeds. They also left for us one of the best examples of customary family life in Muslim history. In this respect, their material and spiritual heritage is a priceless legacy left to us. The Ottoman Empire manifested itself as a civilization of charitable endowments. Because of this, the whole world respected it and it had a very long role in human history.

---

10. *`Asr al-Sa`ada,* "the Age of Happiness," is a term used for the earliest years of Islam.

A Peaceful Home

Q - There have been many institutions founded by Ottoman queens, princesses and other ladies from the palace. Could you give us some information about this?

It is remarkable to note that 1,400 out of the 26,300 confirmed pious foundations were established by eminent women. Among them are several institutions built by *Nur Banu Valide Sultan*[11] on both the Anatolian and the European sides of Istanbul. Uskudar Atik Valide Mosque with its soup kitchen, its college, its hospital and its double bathhouse is very worthy of mention.

Another philanthropic imperial lady was *Mâhpeyker Kösem Vâlide Sultan*. She laid the foundations of New Mosque. She also built Üsküdar Çinili Mosque, as well as a school, a fountain, a hadith college and a double bathhouse next to it. In addition,

---

11. The official epithet for the female members of the Ottman dynasty was *Sultan Efendi*. The title meant that a woman's father was either the sultan himself or one of the sons of the sultan. If such a lady married someone outside the dynasty, their daughters were addressed as *Hanım Sultan* and their sons as *Beyzade*; the mothers themselves were called *Sultanzade*. If *beyzade*s or *sultanzade*s married someone outside the imperial family, their children were not considered part of the imperial family. On the other hand, when the mothers of sultans did not come from the imperial family – they usually did not – then their official epithet was *Valide Sultan*. A sultan's wives were called *Kadın Efendi*. If there were more than one, then ordinal numbers would be added before the epithet.

Some Ottoman Examples

she commissioned the mosque in the district of Anadolu Kavağı intersection. Her endowment for helping poor and orphan girls get married is very famous and there are many others.

Even *Kösem Sultan*, who is known among the Valide Sultans for her temper, took her place among the figures of mercy and compassion by her endowments. Though she laid down the foundations of New Mosque, her life wasn't long enough to finish it. The honor of finishing that mosque belonged to *Hatice Turhan Sultan*, who had other pious deeds such as schools, colleges, soup kitchens, libraries and fountains to her credit. It is worth mentioning that she had honey syrup brought in from the mountains during the month of Ramadan and on other holy nights and offered it to the congregation after the prayers. Even the type of honey to be used was specified in her endowment deeds. In those days, the best quality honey was from a town called Atina, in Rize. It was written in the endowment deed that this type of honey had to be bought, no matter how expensive it was. That detail reveals how sensitive and fine the services offered by charitable endowments often were. This lady left very rich resources for the continuity of service of her endowments and appointed 116 salaried workers for endowment administration.

Pertevniyâl Vâlide Sultan endowed the Valide Mosque in Aksaray, as well as Ya Vedud Mosque. She also commissioned a library, a fountain and a school.

A Peaceful Home

Even though she established numerous institutions, among them the two Selatin Mosques, or Royal Mosques (one in Edirnekapi and one in Uskudar), *Mihrimah Sultan* was a very humble person. Here is the best example manifesting her modesty.

Fresh water had been brought to Mecca and `Arafat by Harun al-Rashid's wife *Zubayda Hanim* a very long time ago. By the time of Sultan Suleiman's reign, however, the channels were broken and rusty. When Mihrimah Sultan learned of the situation, she went to her father, Sultan Suleiman the Magnificent and asked that the old water channels be repaired – in the name of an anonymous donor – by the Sultan's head architect, the famous Sinan. She donated all her ornaments and jewelry for the expenditures. Sinan disappeared for awhile after he had laid down the foundations of Suleymaniye Mosque in Istanbul. The reason for his disappearance wasn't known. One speculation was that he went away so that the foundation of the mosque might settle. But the real reason was to repair the water channels for the Well of Zubayda. This mission remained a secret because of the benefactor's wish.

Another well-known charitable queen mother was *Bezmiâlem Vâlide Sultan*, who left several monumental charitable works behind. Among the mosques she had built, the biggest one is the Valide Mosque located next to Dolmabahce Palace. The world-famous Galata Bridge can also be mentioned among her endowments.

Some Ottoman Examples

The endowment she established in Damascus is also very important. Two of its undertakings were to carry fresh water from Damascus to pilgrims and to replace household items broken by maids, in order to protect the maids' pride and dignity.

Bezmiâlem Vâlide Sultan's another outstanding foundation is the Ghuraba-i Muslimin Hospital, which was built by a significant donation from her private wealth. This monument started giving service, with its mosque and fountain, in 1843 and ever since has been delivering healing to poor members of the Muslim community.

These queen mothers and princesses gave utmost importance to water. They furnished fountains all over Mecca, `Arafat and Istanbul. They built aqueducts that still stand and repaired water canals that long provided abundant water for the entire city of Istanbul.

Our ancestors sincerely established numerous pious foundations, which they prayed would serve people until Judgment Day. These foundations not only met the needs of people in their time: most of them are still offering their services to humanity in every field of social welfare. They are signs of our ancestors' faith, nobility and continuous charity and for these they will always be remembered.

O Allah! Count us among those devoted Muslims who serve creation for the love of the Creator and who duly take care of Your trusts.

Amin!

EPILOGUE

Family life, which began with the creation of human beings, is a mirror reflecting in advance the results of our eternal journey. For family is the first school where a person's emotions, will, reason and soul are educated. It is the location of our first love, our first sharing, our first happiness and our first paradise on earth.

Therefore a blessed home is among the highest goods. Home must be returned to its original state as the center of our lives. While we may well recognize the smallest favors of the people outside our homes with great appreciation, let us not forget the sacrifices and goodness lived out inside those walls. Let family unity not turn into boredom; may spouses always value each other. Indeed, may our family relationships increase their value as time passes, like the magnificent charitable monuments of old.

We must revise our understanding of the whole idea of home. A believer's home cannot be a hotel, or a place where all kinds of heedlessness are committed. It should be a garden of the soul where flowers of love, affection, sharing and service are cultivated.

If we can achieve such families in this world, we can attain eternal happiness in the Hereafter.

In other words, our homes must be places where family members love and support each other, so that we do not run away from each other *on the Day which a man will flee from his brother, his mother and father and his spouse and children.*[12] We should think about what kind of lifestyle might lead us to such a level of spiritual maturity.

In a hadith, the Prophet (peace and blessings be upon him) says:

People die in accordance with how they live and are resurrected in accordance with how they die. (Munawi, *Fayd al-Qadir*, V, 663)

When we establish strong family connections and attachments based on the principles discussed in this work, then our homes will become an eternal reward, as well as a foundation for the building of goodness, tranquility and magnificence throughout our society.

Dear Lord! Bless us with such homes. Draw this great nation and its youth toward eternal happiness in this blessed land. Grant that we may raise up a brave people, resembling those who went before us!
Amin!

---

12. Qur'an 80:34-6

CONTENTS

Foreword 5

Marriage and Family in Islam 9

Things that Women Need to Pay Attention to in the Family 41

Things That Men Need to Pay Attention to in the Family 59

Things that Men and Women Together Need to Pay Attention to in the Family 75

About Child Discipline 91

The Place of Women in Islam and the Education of females 125

Some Ottoman Examples 141

Epilogue 149

ISLAMIC BOOKS IN PDF FORMAT FOR FREE

YOU CAN DOWNLOAD 286 ISLAMIC BOOKS IN 32 LANGUAGES ON INTERNET FOR FREE!

Islamic books in various languages are now waiting for you in pdf format at www.islamicpublishing.net.

You may printout the copies downloaded in pdf formats, reproduce them or send to your loved ones via email.

You may also read the books by visiting the site with your iPad or iPhone devices.

Our campaign of free downloads is for promotion and is limited to 1 year.

To obtain a free copy in pdf of any one of the books, you only need to visit www.islamicpublishing.net web site by clicking to "Catalog" button and by selecting the appropriate language.

English – French – German – Spanish – Italian – Russian – Arabic – Portuguese – Chinese – Traditional Chinese
Hungarian – Ukrainian – Tajik – Albanian – Kazan Tatar – Crimean Tatar – Bulgarian – Uzbek – Bosnian – Kyrgyz – Azeri
Kazakh – Georgian – Bashkir – Uyghur – Ahıska – Hausa – Swahili – Mooré – Luganda – Twi – Wolof

ERKAM PUBLISHING